THE HUMAN ADVANTAGE

HARNESSING THE STRENGTH OF HUMAN
CAPITAL IN AN AI-DRIVEN WORLD

RABI ATITI

Copyright © 2025 Rabi Atiti.

All rights reserved.

ISBN 9798290527079

No part of this book may be reproduced, stored in a retrieval system, or transmitted in any form or by any means without the written permission of the author.

Images used under licence from Canva Pro (www.canva.com) and public domain sources.

Published by Purple Inkshed

25 Coker Street, Ogba, Lagos, Nigeria

+234 903 998 8552

Cover design by Lucent 7 Creatives

+234 814 839 2695

ENDORSEMENTS

'A powerful and essential read that proves in an age of machines, our humanity is our greatest advantage. Rabi lights the way forward, championing empathy, creativity, and courage that are not just soft skills, but strategic imperatives for success.'
—**Mark Breslin,**
Co-founder and Director, Amplifi & Impact AI Consultancy

'Only Rabi could write this – a book grounded in lived experience and global insight, with case studies that break the usual mould. The argument is so well-reasoned and compelling, you're left nodding – and ready to act.'
—**Meera Somji,**
CEO and Founder, Clusivity

'Courage comes in many forms. Rabi Atiti's life displays a passion for life conjoined with the courage to make key decisions that influence and bring change. We believe *The Human Advantage* is a prophetic and anointed 'now word' for leaders across the globe. It is a word of hope, reminding us of the gift of our humanity, and reinforcing the truth that we are much more than machines: we are made in the image of God.'

—**Neil and Hazel Pattison,**
Lead Couple, Jubilee Church Maidstone

'A compelling exploration of what makes us uniquely human in an increasingly technological world. *The Human Advantage* offers profound insights and a refreshing perspective on our enduring capabilities.'

—**Deji Soyemi,**
IT Consultant

'I have known Rabi very closely for over two decades, from being a university student combining education with trading to support herself through school, to the wonderful mother and amiable business leader that she has become. No one is better suited than Rabi to write about what the enormous power of the human advantage brings to all situations of change in our lives and workplaces. This is a story well told and a book well written. A must-read and re-read.'

—**Dr Austin Okogun,**
CEO, Lily Hospitals, Nigeria

'This is a timely book; it is a message of hope that we can turn around or transcend past and present conditions in our lives through courage, determination, and resilience.'

—**Dr Makaziwe Mandela**

'A timely reminder of the human element in a world where artificial intelligence (AI) is leading business and societal development. This book offers insights into aligning human values and ethics with technological innovation. It is essential reading for navigating the future of work and digital transformation.'

—**Misan Jekhine,**
Researcher/Lecturer, Leeds Beckett University

'*The Human Advantage* is an excellent book that is both engaging and deep in its insight. The very positive approach is infectious and is sure to make an impact!'

—**Rebecca Marsh,**
Publisher, Business, Management, & Economics Routledge, Taylor & Francis Group

'I highly recommend *The Human Advantage* by Rabi Atiti, a compelling exploration of how empathy, creativity, and emotional intelligence will define leadership in the digital age. Rabi brings her extensive experience as the Head of Inclusion for EMEA and India at Informa and over 15 years of strategic leadership in DEI, and a passion for building inclusive, high-impact cultures to this topic.'

—**Linda Blackerby,**
Experienced Board Member and Global Commercial P&L Operator

'In a world racing toward automation, *The Human Advantage* is a timely and necessary reminder that our greatest edge isn't digital – it's human. This book offers more than just insight; it offers a roadmap for leading with empathy, creativity, critical thinking, and emotional intelligence (EQ). In a time when technology often overshadows humanity, this is a refreshing, grounded, and necessary guide for leaders who want to create real impact. The book is written by someone who personifies being human.'

—**Ritika Wadhwa,**
Chief Executive Officer, Prabhaav Global (Cultural Intelligence Guru)

'Rabi has a truly engaging writing style – taking the reader by the hand and leading, step-by-step – drawing on a wide range of inputs and insights to create a multi-dimensional set of perspectives and recommendations.'

—**Jeremy North,**
Director of Advanced Learning,
Routledge, Taylor & Francis Group

'Rabi is a fearless advocate for young people and inclusive leadership. *The Human Advantage* challenges us to lead with empathy and emotional intelligence – not ego. It's a timely call to action and a bold manifesto for the kind of leadership today's generation expects – and deserves.'

—**Faheem Khan,**
Founder and CEO, Future Leaders UK

'A great read that solidifies the need for balance in a world dominated by technological advancements. Growth through technology is vital, but not at the cost of the human connection. A well-balanced narration of how choice and discernment keep us unique.'

—**Melissa Watson,**
Informa Plc Group Operations Director

'An objective look at the emergence and importance of AI and yet with a balanced view of how a human-centric approach to engaging with AI remains the X factor in innovative breakthroughs. A must read for anyone who relies on technology to shape their teams, business, organisation, and most importantly, their workforce or employees.'

—**Siji and Ibi Otenigbagbe,**
Business Change Professional and Entrepreneur

'The Human Advantage is a remarkable work by Rabi Atiti, whose contribution to AI is both insightful and transformative. With clarity and precision, Rabi communicates complex ideas, blending theoretical depth, practical application, and ethical reflection in a way that educates and inspires. This book sparks meaningful conversations about the future of technology and human potential, making it an indispensable resource for all.'

—**Dr Edna Abibetu Abidde,**
PhD in Guidance and Counselling
Head of department, Senior Lecturer, College of Education

'Rabi Atiti's writing style is relatable, relevant, inspiring – and so very human, driving her point about our role in the age of AI. Our human advantage is irreplaceable, and *The Human Advantage* will help readers see it in themselves.'

—**Danica Cullins,**
Executive Vice President of Health and Nutrition, Informa, Platinum Sponsor of Women in Nutraceuticals (WIN)

DEDICATION

This book is dedicated to my children, Sadetu, Kayla, and Keslar, whose futures will be shaped by the decisions we make today.

Contents

Author's Note	XIII
Preface	XVI
Introduction	1
1. The Myth of Inevitable Obsolescence	10
2. The Business Case for Humanity	21
3. The Real Competitive Edge	34
4. Leading with Humanity in the Digital Age	47
5. The Future of Leadership	60
6. Emotional Intelligence	72
7. The Global Power of Inclusion	84
8. Agility Versus Burnout	101
9. Resilience and Reinvention	121
10. Designing the Future of Work Around Humans	134
11. Time Together: An Informa Case Study	151
12. Building Psychological Resilience	160
13. Leveraging Technology	172

Conclusion	184
Acknowledgements	197
Appendix	199
Endnotes	203

Author's Note

When I began this book, I was resisting more than I was writing. I was resisting the speed of change – resisting the growing presence of technology in our lives and resisting the fear that we were losing something essential – something human along the way.

I had the language of inclusion, the heart for people, and the appetite for change, but I was still wary of tech. Especially AI. A part of me was holding back. Yet, in that tension, between resistance and realisation – this book was born.

As I shaped the final chapters, I received a message from one of my mentors, who had just finished reading the advance copy. His feedback stopped me in my tracks. Not only was it kind – it was thoughtful, challenging, and deeply affirming. It humbled me to my core.

My mentor reminded me of something I often tell others: 'Data may inform us, but it's stories that move us.' In my effort to ground this book in credible research and respected case studies, I realised I had at times leant too far into the analyst's voice, and in doing so, I risked dimming the light of the one thing that truly sets this work apart: my lived experience.

From a tech-resistant mother, struggling to stay connected, to an inclusion leader embracing AI, not as a threat, but as a tool to elevate humanity. This has always been a story of growth, of courage, of learning to turn vulnerability into strength.

My mentor encouraged me to share more of that journey, especially the moments of uncertainty, the quiet doubts, and the steep learning curve. He was correct, because this book isn't about having all the answers. It's about showing that in the age of AI, it will take our shared humanity, anchored in courage and wisdom, to ask the right questions and challenge ourselves.

There is a powerful, often untold story that bridges the reluctant tech-resistor in the preface to the AI enthusiast I am now. This is a journey marked by curiosity, discomfort, reflection, and growth.

In a moment of professional curiosity, and with no small amount of courage, I reached out to Mark Breslin, who had once invited me to bring an inclusion lens to the Elysia project at Informa. This time, I asked him to be my AI mentor. To my surprise and deep gratitude, he said yes.

What followed was a quiet, transformative journey. Mark challenged me to stretch my thinking, to take courses, to stay open. He made space for my questions and never once made me feel behind. Slowly, my fear gave way to fascination.

There were moments I sat in awe of what AI could do; how it could unlock time, spark creativity, and even deepen inclusion when used wisely, with intention, care, and balance. That journey from 'Where do I even start?' *to* confidently advocating for human-centred AI is one of the most profound shifts I've experienced in my career.

One of my early readers wrote:

'Your story is not just the beating heart of the book – it's your greatest strategic asset.' So, I gave it permission to breathe. The hard lessons. The resistance. The reinvention. The rawness and the learning that followed.

This book is not a manual. It's not a how-to guide. It's a call to courage, a call to lead, listen, and learn differently. To embrace technology, not as a replacement for human connection, but to amplify what makes us most human. This underpins my goal of giving 50 per cent of proceeds from the sale of *The Human Advantage* to help STEM students in Nigeria, Rwanda and the UK.

If somewhere in these pages you see fragments of yourself – in my hesitation, my hope, or the messy middle – I want you to know that's intentional. That's where the learning lives, because at its core, this book was never just about AI, or inclusion, or even leadership. It's about *us* and the dividend we all stand to gain when we choose to lead with humanity.

Rabi Atiti

Preface

There was a time when technology innovation held no allure for me. It was cold and stripped of the warmth and complexity that define human relationships. To me, technology was something that took away instead of giving, that distanced more often than connected. For years, this distance was more personal than philosophical, deeply rooted in experiences that shaped my earliest views of the role of technology in our lives.

My journey into this world didn't start with curiosity; it began with resistance, frustration, and even resentment. I spent two decades of my life with a brilliant tech genius whose passion for information technology (IT) and innovation eclipsed anything that my mind could comprehend. Technology was not just his work; it was his world and made it our world. Our home became a laboratory of gadgets and innovations, advanced enough to fascinate, intrusive enough to alienate. The more connected we became digitally, the more disconnected we felt emotionally. It seemed we had allowed technology to invade the precious space reserved for family, for intimacy, for simple human conversation.

One memory stays vividly with me: the early 2000s, during the implementation of Systems, Applications, and Products (SAP) at Shell Petroleum Development Company (SPDC) Nigeria. I remember accompanying my ex-husband to those late-night meetings, feeling distant and frustrated, unable to see why this digital world held such a priority over our family life. It wasn't until we relocated to the United Kingdom, thousands of miles away from our support network of family and friends, that this void became glaring. Isolation turned into loneliness, loneliness into resentment, and resentment into a stark declaration – I hated technology. It felt as though technology had stolen from me, and I blamed it for everything.

However, life, as it often does, revealed its complexity in ways I could never anticipate. Years later, through reflection, pain, and a determination to rise above resentment, I discovered something profound: the problem wasn't technology itself – it was the absence of balance. I began to see how innovation could indeed amplify human potential rather than diminish it, but only if guided by empathy, emotional intelligence, ethics, cultural awareness, and genuine human connection.

Today, my relationship with technology has come full circle. I find myself inspired and energised, not as a technologist, but as a human strategist harnessing my lived experience to champion a nuanced and balanced use of AI, leveraging the unique strengths of both human wisdom and tech innovation. I've learned from exceptional mentors who exemplify balance, integrating technology with humanity, professional drive with personal fulfilment, innovation with inclusivity. Now, I embrace AI enthusiastically, intentionally, guided by a deep belief that technology should always serve humanity, enhance our connections, and elevate our collective experience.

This transformation inspired me to write *The Human Advantage*, a book born from real world insights and countless conversations during my global listening tours. Everywhere, from boardrooms to local communities, I've heard the same underlying concerns: fear of displacement, concerns about bias, apprehension around losing the very essence of what makes us human. Yet alongside those fears, I've found curiosity, openness, and a genuine hunger for knowledge – people longing to understand not just what AI can do, but why it matters and how it can shape our lives positively.

I have embraced this calling, to act as a bridge, connecting the world of human experience with tech innovation. My vision is clear: I aim to advocate for AI that respects and celebrates human diversity, proactively addresses ethical blind spots, elevates culturally relevant applications, and equips leaders to build trust, not just technology.

This is my journey; a journey of rebellion turned into resilience, and of silence transformed into strength. It's a narrative that reminds us all that our greatest advantage is inherently human.

At this critical intersection of AI, automation, and constant change, I'm convinced more deeply than ever that the future will not simply belong to those who master codes or algorithms. It will belong to leaders who foster community, champion inclusion, lead with empathy, and innovate for meaningful impact, not just efficiency.

The future belongs to those who remember that innovation without integrity is empty, that leadership without empathy is incomplete, and that progress without humanity is meaningless.

This is *The Human Advantage* – it belongs to all of us.

Introduction

With algorithms predicting behaviour, machines surpassing human processing power, and automation threatening industries, keeping up with technology can easily feel like a race. But what if I told you that the true edge – the real competitive advantage – doesn't lie in machines, but in the irreplaceable qualities of being human?

No machine, however advanced, can replicate the human advantage – a collection of uniquely human, inherent traits. It's empathy in leadership, creativity in innovation, critical thinking in decision making and emotional intelligence in collaboration. These aren't just soft skills; they're strategic assets. They're what will differentiate the average from the exceptional in the age of AI, automation, and constant disruption.

While technology may accelerate efficiency, it can't replicate compassion. It can simulate patterns, but not imagination. It can process data, but it can't make ethical decisions rooted in lived experience. Machines can be programmed; humans can dream. Therein lies the advantage.

Why Now?

With AI automation reshaping jobs and workforce expectations, shifting traditional leadership and breaking down models, businesses must rethink their approach to people, performance, and culture. *The Human Advantage* will serve as the go-to leadership playbook for building resilient, high-performing and future-ready organisations.

We're at a tipping point. The Fourth Industrial Revolution has brought AI, machine learning, big data, and robotics into the mainstream. In boardrooms and governments alike, decisions are being made at breakneck speed to digitise, automate and optimise activities. But what often gets left behind in this race for technological supremacy is the recognition that machines are tools, not replacements for human potential. Over the years, we've seen the dangers of leaning too heavily on automation without questioning the bias coded into algorithms and witnessed the fatigue of digital overload, the erosion of trust and the loss of human connection.

The Human Advantage reminds us that technology should serve people, not the other way around. It's not about competing with machines but complementing them with uniquely human strengths.

The Four Cornerstones of the Human Advantage

Let's briefly introduce the four essential human qualities at the heart of this concept:

1. **Empathy**
   This is the ability to understand and share the feelings of

another. In leadership, empathy builds trust, inclusion, and psychological safety. Machines may read sentiment analysis, but they don't feel. Empathy allows us to connect, lead authentically, and navigate complex social dynamics.

2. **Creativity**

While AI can remix existing ideas, humans imagine new ones. Creativity drives innovation, problem-solving and differentiation. It's how organisations evolve and how societies progress.

3. **Critical Thinking**

In an era where information overload is the norm, the ability to question, analyse and make sound judgements is priceless. Critical thinking is the antidote to misinformation, unconscious bias, and reactive decision-making. It allows leaders to see beyond data, challenge assumptions and envision new possibilities.

4. **Emotional Intelligence (EQ)**

Simply put, it is the capacity to recognise, understand and manage emotions, both yours and others'. High EQ fosters collaboration, adaptability, and resilience. It turns a group of individuals into a cohesive, high-performing team.

Beyond Business: A Global Perspective

The Human Advantage doesn't stop at the individual or organisational level. It extends to the wider society. As countries grapple with socio-political divides, climate change, and technological disruption, leaders who prioritise humanity and recognise the value of inclusion, compassion, and shared progress will shape more sustainable, resilient futures. In short, empathy, creativity, and EQ scale, but this happens only when we choose to centre them.

This book is for professionals, companies, and countries alike. It's a manifesto, a guide, and a challenge to rethink success, not as a product of technology alone, but as a result of how we leverage the very qualities that make us human.

Throughout these chapters, I'll share stories, strategies, and research that show how empathy, creativity, critical thinking and emotional intelligence have transformed leaders, businesses, and societies over the years. You'll see how these traits are not just *nice-to-haves* but *must-haves* – the currency of leadership in the future of work, innovation, and inclusion.

So, as you turn each page, ask yourself: how are you embracing your human advantage? How are you creating space for others to do the same?

We stand at the dawn of a new industrial revolution, one not driven by steam or silicon alone, but by the seamless partnership between humans and machines. Algorithms now sift through billions of data points in the blink of an eye; yet behind every breakthrough in AI is a uniquely human spark: curiosity, empathy, and the courage to ask 'Why?'

In today's world, it's tempting to believe that technology will render our soft skills obsolete. After all, your smartwatch can track your heart rate, while a chatbot can handle your frequently asked questions (FAQs) emails. But ask yourself: who coaches the coach? Who writes the next great strategic narrative? Who senses when a team member needs encouragement or when a project is veering off course? Those are questions no machine can answer because they require emotional intelligence, creative problem-solving and the ability to weave meaning into the mundane.

Let's face it, spreadsheets don't tell jokes, nor does code offer a shoulder to lean on; yet these human touches are precisely what turn good businesses into beloved institutions. When leaders listen, when teams collaborate across cultures, and when organisations embrace kindness as a strategic asset, they unlock levels of engagement and innovation that no amount of automation can replicate.

The Human Advantage is your guide to harnessing this power. Within these pages, you'll find:

- **Evidence-based insights** on why empathy and creativity drive performance in an AI-enabled economy.

- **Vivid case studies** of companies that have turned human-centric leadership into measurable growth.

- **Practical strategies** for cultivating emotional intelligence, critical thinking, and adaptability both in yourself and in your teams.

From Nigeria to New Zealand ... From Silicon Valley to Singapore, *The Human Advantage* includes 28 **unique case studies** spanning 17 **countries** across various regions.

Case studies and countries featured:

1. United Kingdom (UK)

Informa – Leadership during Covid-19 & Time Together

Bain & Company – Inclusive leadership practices (UK & Global)

NHS – Psychological safety and culture transformation

2. United States of America (USA)

Microsoft – Empathy-led leadership & AI ethics

NVIDIA – Innovation and human creativity in AI

Eli Lilly – Human-centred leadership in pharma

Airbnb – Ethical AI and trust

Southwest Airlines – Culture as a competitive edge

Costco – Leadership and employee care

Chobani – Inclusion & refugee hiring

Accenture (also Global) – Human-first leadership in consulting

3. Nigeria

Lily Hospital – Healthcare transformation

Local leadership examples on inclusion and community impact

4. India

Tata Group – Purpose-led business and inclusion

Regional leadership stories within hybrid work context

5. Kenya

Safaricom – Financial inclusion through M-Pesa

Dr. Kakenya Ntaiya – Education and empowerment of girls

6. Denmark

Lego – From near bankruptcy to global reinvention

7. Singapore

Digital innovation and inclusive leadership (example referenced in tech sector)

8. Australia

Atlassian – Culture, psychological safety, distributed trust

9. New Zealand

Case highlighting distributed leadership practices

10. South Africa

Leadership adaptation in post-pandemic realities (referenced case)

11. United Arab Emirates (UAE)

Dubai Leadership Talks – Accessibility and inclusion as competitive advantage

12. Taiwan

Audrey Tang – Digital democracy and transparency

13. Brazil

Semco – Radical organisational democracy

Natura – Sustainable leadership and inclusion

14. Turkey

Chobani (origins in Turkey, expanded to USA)

15. Canada

Referenced in AI & inclusion contexts (case study)

16. China

Referenced in global supply chain & innovation case

17. Saudi Arabia (KSA) Referenced in leadership and transformation section

The Human Advantage is more than a book; it's a global journey through the power of human intelligence and imagination to shape the future of work by leveraging AI wisely.

Across 17 countries and 28 real-world case studies, I've explored how the most human-centred organisations are not just surviving in the age of AI; they're thriving *because of* their people. Whether it's Lily Hospital in Nigeria preparing for AI-assisted diagnostics, Microsoft's cultural turnaround built on empathy, Bain & Company's consistency in connection, the cultural revolution in Kenya, Informa's COVID-19 response prioritising well-being and psychological safety, or what Glassdoor insights are telling us about what people truly value at work, each story reaffirms one truth: **When we lead with humanity, we unlock exponential impact.**

The Human Advantage is a call to reimagine leadership, culture, and technology through a human lens, because machines alone won't build the future. It will be shaped by humans who know how to partner with them **wisely**.

Whether you're an executive grappling with hybrid-work dynamics, a human resource (HR) leader seeking to build inclusive cultures or an aspiring entrepreneur curious about the intersection of tech and humanity, this book will equip you with the tools to shape the future of business, one human interaction at a time.

So, let's get started.

'The machines are ready to crunch numbers; it's on us to give those numbers soul.'—Rabi Atiti.

1

THE MYTH OF INEVITABLE OBSOLESCENCE

We are witnessing the most disruptive shift in human history. 'AI is coming for your job!' is no longer a sensational headline, warning of a future disruption; we are living in its reality. The question is: should this really be a disruption that displaces humans?

In the late 19th and early 20th centuries, horse-drawn vehicles were the primary mode of transportation in New York City. A notable example is the photograph below of Fifth Avenue on Easter Sunday in 1900, where the street is teeming with horse-drawn carriages and only a single automobile is visible. By 1913, just 13 years later, the same avenue had undergone a significant shift, with automobiles dominating the scene and only a few horse-drawn carriages remaining.

Another 1917 image shows Manhattan's horse-drawn carriages in their final days, depicting a city street full of them, just before motorised transport replaced them.

Today, New York City's streets are characterised by cars, taxis, and buses. Photographs of modern-day Manhattan showcase avenues lined with yellow cabs and private vehicles, reflecting the city's shift towards motorised transportation.

This transformation from horse-drawn carriages to automobiles illustrates the rapid technological and infrastructural changes that have shaped New York City's urban landscape over the past century.

Innovations have become a part of our human existence. It is how we fine-tune our world's operating system. However, we are left with a lingering fear in the form of a question: 'Will this invention make humans obsolete?' This fear has throbbed beneath the surface of man's existence from the first assembly lines to today's AI, machine learning and automation for as long as humans have innovated.

Headlines scream, 'AI is coming for your job!' Commentators warn of 'The Rise of the Machines.' Yet, beneath this anxiety lies a myth – a seductive, oversimplified story. The truth? Humans are not and will not be replaceable. What's shifting isn't the need for human contribution, but *how* that contribution is valued and leveraged.

The False Narrative of Replacement

Let's pause for a minute and ask ourselves this question: what can AI do? AI can process vast datasets trained and curated by humans at a speed and scale we simply can't match. It can analyse, identify patterns, automate tasks and optimise with impressive efficiency. However, the question remains: what can AI not do?

AI cannot understand nuance or context in the way humans do. It doesn't feel emotions, doesn't empathise, or intuit. It cannot make ethical or moral judgement independently. AI struggles to adapt to completely novel situations or interpret environments beyond the data it's been trained on.

Yes, AI is undeniably powerful. Its ability to integrate and process vast streams of information at speed is remarkable. However, our uniquely human qualities – cognitive depth, emotional intelligence, moral reasoning and ethical awareness make us truly extraordinary and irreplaceable.

AI is a tool, not a replacement. The future doesn't belong to AI alone; it belongs to the humans who know how to harness its power and partner with it wisely, with clarity and purpose.

How to Leverage AI to Empower You

1. **Position yourself for this shift:** Use AI to augment your creativity, critical thinking, empathy, and cultural intelligence – skills AI can't replicate at scale.

2. **Automate the mundane, elevate the meaningful:** Let AI take over repetitive tasks (e.g., research, data synthesis, scheduling) to allow you to focus on vision, relationships, and strategy.

3. **Build your AI fluency:** You don't need to code, but understanding prompts, ethical boundaries, data bias, and application frameworks makes you a better AI leader, not a passive user.

4. **Stay deeply human:** The more AI automates, the more valuable distinctly human qualities become, like trust, wisdom, and moral courage.

Historical Perspective: We've Seen This Before

Let's rewind to the Industrial Revolution. Textile machines threatened to put weavers out of work. The Luddites, fearing for their livelihoods, destroyed the machines. But the outcome was nuanced: while some jobs were lost, entirely new industries and roles emerged.[1]

Fast forward to the digital age: automated teller machines (ATMs) were predicted to replace bank tellers entirely. Instead, the number of tellers grew. Why? Automation freed them from mundane tasks, allowing for focus on relationship-building, financial advising, and problem-solving – skills ATMs could never master.

Bank of America and the Human Element

In 2019, Bank of America launched 'Advanced Centres' filled with ATMs and AI-powered chatbots. However, they deliberately increased and trained human employee to offer personalised financial advice.[2] The result? Higher customer satisfaction and increased client retention. Technology handled transactions, but humans handled trust and connection.

Here's the crux: machines excel at efficiency, repetition, and data crunching. But they lack what I call the 'Human Quadrant':

- **Empathy**
- **Ethical Judgement**
- **Contextual Creativity**

- **Complex Collaboration**

AI can simulate a conversation. It cannot replicate a genuine human connection. It can generate options but cannot make ethical decisions influenced by culture, lived experiences, or empathy.

The Boeing 737 MAX Case

A case where over-reliance on automated systems without adequate human oversight led to catastrophic failures – a reminder that technology without human ethical judgement is not just incomplete; it can be dangerous.[3]

The Business Case: Human-Centric Companies Win

If you examine the leading companies that are thriving in today's marketplace, you will observe a fascinating pattern of success: they top the charts of companies that are prioritising human-centric leadership strategies, making significant investments in their workforce and fostering a strong sense of belonging and connection with their team.

Case Study: Microsoft's Cultural Transformation Under Satya Nadella

Nadella didn't just focus on cloud computing or AI – he reinvented Microsoft's culture around empathy, collaboration and growth mindset. Employee engagement skyrocketed. So did innovation. The result? Microsoft became the world's most valuable company in 2024 because it recognised the irreplaceable value of human adaptability and empathy, alongside tech advancement.[4]

Emerging Evidence: AI + Humans = Super Teams

A study conducted by researchers at the Massachusetts Institute of Technology (MIT) has revealed that the most effective and productive approach involves collaboration between humans and AI rather than substituting human workers with AI systems, leading to superior results.[5]

- AI alone: 60-70 per cent accuracy

- Humans alone: 70-80 per cent accuracy

- AI + Human: Over 90 per cent accuracy

IBM Watson might scan millions of medical journals, but patients prefer diagnoses discussed by doctors who can translate information into compassionate care.

The Irreplaceable Human Advantage

The myth of obsolescence thrives on fear. But history, data, and human experience give good grounds to discount that fear because machines can only automate tasks and humans elevate value. When we lean into our empathy, creativity, and collaboration, we unlock competitive advantages that no algorithm can replicate. This strengthens the reality that the future isn't human *vs.* machine. It's human *with* machine led by humans.

Practical strategies for amplifying the human advantage in an AI-driven world begin with redesigning roles around uniquely human skills. Rather than structuring jobs around routine tasks, forward-thinking leaders should intentionally reshape roles to prioritise emotional intelligence. This includes encouraging relationship-building, negotiation, and mentoring. Equally vital is fostering creative problem-solving by focusing on complex challenges involving multiple variables, diverse perspectives, and ambiguity. Teams should be empowered to co-create policies and systems that reflect human values. In practical terms, this means conducting a 'task audit' within teams – categorising tasks into those suitable for automation and those that require human judgement. The latter should be transitioned into formal key performance indicators (KPIs) – such as quality of collaboration, client trust, and creative contributions.

Invest in Human-Centric Learning and Development

Companies often spend heavily on tech upskilling, but less on human-centric capabilities. Let's examine below some proven approaches that foster human-centric learning and development.

Empathy labs: regular workshops using role-play, perspective-shifting exercises and exposure to diverse lived experiences.

Critical thinking clinics: programmes teaching Socratic questioning, logical fallacies, and decision-making under uncertainty.

Creativity hackathons: cross-disciplinary innovation challenges encouraging lateral thinking, rewarded not for efficiency, but for originality. An apt example that comes to mind is Salesforce's 'Ohana Culture': Their emphasis on emotional intelligence training and mindfulness programmes is cited as a core reason for high employee engagement and retention, despite high levels of tech integration.[6]

Build Human-Machine Collaboration Teams (Super Teams)

Instead of isolating AI specialists from human teams, they should be integrated to work in tandem. In practice, this means appointing 'Collaboration Architects' – professionals who ensure that AI tools enhance rather than dictate workflows. Leadership development programmes should also include AI literacy training – focusing not only on technical proficiency but also on understanding AI's limitations, risks, and ethical implications. For instance, Unilever uses AI for initial candidate screening, but always relies on humans to conduct final interviews, safeguarding fairness, human judgement, and cultural fit.

Embed Ethical Governance Structures

Machines have no moral compass; it is up to humans to supply one. In practical terms, this means establishing ethical AI councils – diverse, multi-disciplinary groups tasked with reviewing how algorithms are deployed and monitored. Leaders must also undergo AI bias and inclusion audits to ensure that human oversight can identify and correct unintended biases in automated systems. For example, Airbnb's ethical commitment initiative introduced explicit bias-checking mechanisms within its AI booking systems, guided by a dedicated human ethics team. This move helped restore public trust after previous discrimination issues came to light. Ultimately, the individuals and organisations that will thrive are not those who fear or resist AI, but those who courageously redesign their systems, policies, and cultures around a central truth: technology is a tool, but humanity is the differentiator.

When we lean into our empathy, creativity, and collaboration, we unlock competitive advantages that no algorithm can replicate.

2

THE BUSINESS CASE FOR HUMANITY

In a world where competitive advantage is increasingly tied to intangible assets like human talent and culture, investing in people has become a strategic imperative. Intangible assets (such as human capital, innovation, and brand) now comprise about 90 per cent of the Standard and Poor (S&P) 500's market value, reflecting how critical workforce capabilities and culture are to business success. Forward-thinking companies treat their people as core assets – not costs, and research shows these human-centred companies financially outperform their peers.

This chapter presents compelling global data and cross-industry case studies, demonstrating that prioritising people isn't a 'soft' strategy, but a hard driver of profit and growth. From higher profitability linked to inclusive cultures to multi-fold returns on well-being and leadership investments, the evidence confirms that putting humans at the heart of business pays off.

People-Centric Cultures Drive Performance

Leading research consultancies have gathered data that link human-centred workplace cultures to stronger business performance. A Gallup meta-analysis covering over 100,000 teams worldwide found that highly engaged teams (top quartile in engagement) achieve 23 per cent greater profitability than those with low engagement. They also see 10 per cent higher customer loyalty, 18 per cent higher productivity, and significantly lower turnover. Despite this, only 23 per cent of global employees were engaged in 2022, leaving vast untapped potential.

Gallup estimates that low engagement and active disengagement cost the world $8.8 trillion in lost productivity – nine per cent of global gross domestic product (GDP). In short, companies that activate employee commitment and well-being reap tangible rewards, while neglecting the human element leads to steep financial losses.[1]

Research also highlights the business value of diversity, equity, and inclusion (DEI). McKinsey's studies show that companies with more diverse leadership teams enjoy higher profitability. In 2019, organisations in the top quartile for gender diversity were 25 per cent more likely to have above-average profits, while those with higher ethnic and cultural diversity outperformed the bottom quartile by 36 per cent in profitability.[2] Deloitte's findings mirror this: inclusive cultures have 27 per cent higher profitability, 22 per cent greater productivity, and 39 per cent higher customer satisfaction. In other words, fostering a culture of belonging is not just a moral choice but a clear business advantage.

Organisational culture has become a critical factor for resilience and success, especially during times of disruption. A global PricewaterhouseCooper (PwC) survey of 3,200 leaders and employees across 40+ countries found that 69 per cent of senior leaders credited much of their success during the pandemic to their culture. Nearly 70 per cent said their ability to adapt during crises was rooted in culture as a competitive advantage. 66 per cent of C-suite executives believe culture is more important to performance than strategy or operating model. These leaders found that organisations with people-oriented cultures were more likely to experience revenue growth and higher customer and employee satisfaction during 2020-21. The takeaway: culture 'eats strategy for breakfast', while human-centred cultures drive agility and sustainable performance.

Investors are also recognising workforce metrics as key indicators of long-term value. Analysis by index providers reveals that companies on the *Fortune* '100 Best Companies to Work For' list, known for healthy people practices, have dramatically outperformed the stock market.

Over recent decades, these companies' portfolios would have earned 3.6 times the returns of the overall market. In 2024, the Fortune 100 Best achieved a 41.6 per cent total return, outperforming the Russell 1000 Index by 15.6 percentage points. This suggests that employee experience and culture are crucial to shareholder value. With human capital now seen as a key asset class and social factors rising in environmental, social and governance (ESG), companies can no longer afford to treat people strategy as ancillary, as it is central to competitive advantage.

The People-First Advantage

Real-world case studies across sectors and regions clearly demonstrate how prioritising employees leads to business success. In the technology sector, Microsoft's cultural transformation under Chief Executive Officer (CEO) Satya Nadella is a prime example. When Nadella took over in 2014, he shifted Microsoft's culture from internal competition to one of empathy, collaboration and a 'growth mindset'. One of his first actions was to ask top executives to read a book on 'empathic collaboration', signalling a focus on listening and learning. This human-centred approach sparked innovation and contributed to a market value increase of over $250 billion within a few years.

By breaking silos and emphasising emotional intelligence, Nadella unlocked exceptional performance, turning Microsoft from a stagnant giant into one of the world's most valuable firms. This transformation shows that leading with empathy and purpose can drive significant financial returns, even in competitive tech markets.

In retail, Costco offers a compelling example of the 'people-first' philosophy. It has long invested in its frontline workers with higher wages, better benefits and stable schedules, defying the typical low-cost retail model. The results speak for themselves: Costco pays an average of $26 per hour – well above industry standards – and has an impressively low turnover rate of around 8 per cent, compared to the 60 per cent turnover seen at other retailers.

This loyal, well-trained workforce drives higher productivity and customer service, leading to sales per employee nearly three times higher than Walmart's. Co-founder Jim Sinegal often said that paying employees well is not altruism but 'good business'.³ Costco's stock consistently outperformed retail peers and the S&P 500 for decades, proving Wall Street sceptics wrong. Its strategy shows that investing in employee well-being leads to lower turnover, fewer errors and higher profits, setting a powerful example for competitors like Sam's Club, which eventually raised wages after seeing the link between pay, turnover, productivity, and competitiveness.

The principle of putting employees first extends to service industries as well. Southwest Airlines, known for its employee-centric culture, enjoyed 47 consecutive years of profitability – an unmatched streak in commercial aviation – prior to the 2020 pandemic. Founder Herb Kelleher's mantra, 'Happy employees create happy customers', shaped Southwest's focus on avoiding layoffs, empowering employees, and fostering a fun, team-oriented environment.⁴ This approach paid off with loyal employees who went the extra mile to provide reliable, friendly service, resulting in the lowest customer complaint rates and a devoted customer base.

Competitors who focused solely on cost-cutting learnt the hard way that eroding employee morale can hurt the customer experience and financial outcomes, as seen in the airline industry's wave of bankruptcies. Even with new pressures today, experts warn that abandoning Southwest's people-first ethos would hurt shareholders in the long run. Southwest's story proves that a culture-driven approach can provide a lasting competitive advantage.

A similar case comes from India's IT services sector. Under CEO Vineet Nayar, HCL Technologies turned the traditional hierarchy on its head with the philosophy of 'Employees First, Customers Second'.

Nayar believed that empowering and enabling employees, particularly those on the frontline, would drive superior customer value. He introduced radical transparency and reversed the accountability model, making managers answerable to employees.[5]

Despite initial scepticism, HCL's revenues and market capitalisation grew six-fold in the first five years of the 'Employees First' programme. The company was also recognised as a top employer across multiple regions. By tapping into the initiative and creativity of its workforce, HCL out-innovated and out-delivered many competitors, showing that an engaged workforce is key to driving customer satisfaction and profits. This case challenges the traditional notion that customers always come first, revealing that nurturing employees enables them to better serve customers, fuelling a cycle of success.

These examples from tech, retail, aviation and IT highlight a key insight: when leadership prioritises a people-first culture, business outcomes improve. Whether through empathy-driven innovation, good jobs strategies, strong service cultures or inverted hierarchies, focusing on employees boosts loyalty, effort, and innovation, leading to better financial results.

These benefits apply across industries and regions, showing that human-centred principles work universally. While specific practices may differ (e.g., Microsoft's growth mindset vs. Costco's wage investment), the core idea remains: investing in people drives value creation and strong returns.

Return on Investment in Inclusion, Well-Being, Engagement, and Leadership

Sceptics often question the 'ROI' of people programmes, but data shows investments in inclusion, wellness, and leadership development yield strong returns. Deloitte research shows inclusive cultures reduce turnover and boost productivity by 22 per cent. Employees who feel valued stay longer and contribute more, while inclusivity expands the talent pool and fosters innovation, with 83 per cent of millennials more engaged in inclusive environments. Diversity in leadership correlates with a 25–36 per cent higher profitability, proving inclusive leadership is a business necessity.[6]

Workforce well-being, often dismissed as a 'soft' issue, has a measurable financial impact. Burnout and mental ill-health drive absenteeism and turnover, costing billions. World Health Organisation (WHO) estimates depression and anxiety cost $1 trillion globally in lost productivity.[7] But supporting mental health pays off: Deloitte found a £4.70 return for every £1 spent in the UK. Well-being programmes boost resilience, engagement, and loyalty, yet only 1–2 per cent of organisations measure ROI in this area, missing a major opportunity to enhance human capital productivity.

Leadership development delivers strong gains too. A 2023 Better Manager Study found a $7 return per $1 spent, with 42 per cent of companies reporting revenue increases from leadership training. Even during downturns, 84 per cent maintained or increased leadership development investments, recognising it as a 'profit multiplier'.

Across inclusion, well-being, engagement, and leadership, the message is clear: investing in people drives measurable ROI. Forward-thinking companies treat these initiatives with the same rigour as operations, tracking KPIs to prove their value. As Deloitte advises, 'if you treasure it, measure it'.[8] The so-called 'soft' stuff produces real, hard results, improving work life and business outcomes alike.

Debunking the 'Soft Strategy' Myth

Despite growing evidence, some executives still view people-focused strategies as a nice-to-have, especially under pressure for short-term results. This outdated view is dangerous. Ignoring workforce engagement and well-being is like neglecting maintenance on a revenue-generating asset, as breakdowns and poor performance follow. In today's economy, people create value, while neglecting people strategies leads to decline.

A common misconception is that spending on culture, learning, or wellness drains profits. The data shows under-investing in people costs more in the long run. For example, high employee turnover, often seen as unavoidable, quietly drains millions in recruiting, productivity loss, and training costs. Investing in engagement, fair pay, and career development can save more than it costs, while preserving knowledge and customer relationships.

Similarly, diversity and inclusion programmes are not just for compliance or public relations (PR); they drive better decisions and higher revenues. Sidelining DEI means leaving money on the table. The actual risk is failing to adapt. Companies that view inclusion as a 'luxury' risk losing their competitive edge in innovation and talent attraction.

An outdated notion is labelling people initiatives as 'soft' because their outcomes aren't immediately quantifiable, like cost-cutting measures. But modern analytics are changing this. Companies now use employee surveys, performance data and human-capital metrics that correlate with financial outcomes. For example, 'organisational health' (a mix of culture and capabilities) has been linked to long-term financial performance. Advanced firms treat culture and talent as leading indicators, not afterthoughts.

With the rise of ESG investing, boards are being asked about workforce well-being and culture, making these material disclosures. Companies like Unilever, Salesforce, and PepsiCo link employee engagement to innovation and customer satisfaction in their investor reports, showing that 'shareholder value' is tied to how a company treats its people. The old hard vs. soft metrics divide is fading; excelling at 'soft' factors is the only sustainable path to deliver hard results.

In the 20th century industrial era, labour was seen as interchangeable, allowing for short-term gains by cutting costs. In the 21st century, where creativity and agility drive success, that mindset is a liability. Human-centred strategies are about enabling performance, not coddling employees. Engaged, healthy employees create more value. As Jack Welch said, 'You need a hard approach to the soft stuff, because the soft stuff drives the hard results.'[9] This means rigorously managing culture, listening to employees, investing in growth and holding leaders accountable for people metrics essential for execution excellence.

Companies stuck in a 'people are costs' mindset will fall behind those who unlock human capital's full potential.

People as the Engine of Sustainable Growth

The weight of research and real-world examples presented in this chapter leads to an undeniable conclusion: investing in people is a core driver of competitive advantage and sustainable growth. Far from being a charitable or secondary concern, human-centred strategies produce measurably better financial outcomes, from profitability and revenue growth to innovation and shareholder returns. Whether through more inclusive leadership teams yielding higher profits, more engaged employees driving customer loyalty and sales or healthier, well-trained workforces delivering productivity gains and cost savings, the story is consistent: prioritising people pays off in performance.

For CEOs, boards, and investors, this is a strategic insight of the highest order. Culture and talent are not 'soft' topics to delegate or delay; they are strategic levers to actively pull. As the PwC Culture Survey noted, companies that treated culture as a differentiator were better able to adapt, innovate and thrive amid the pandemic.

In dynamic, uncertain markets, the organisations that will endure are those with resilient, empowered people and cohesive cultures. Conversely, firms that neglect their people may enjoy a temporary bump by cutting costs or pushing harder, but they eventually face crises, like an inability to execute strategy, a customer exodus because of poor service, or a talent drain that stymies innovation.

Measuring and communicating the ROI of people initiatives to inform enterprise strategy is the mandate for HR and talent professionals. For corporate strategists and board members, the task is to embed human capital considerations into every major decision, be it a merger (will cultures mesh?), a tech deployment (how will it augment employees?) or a market expansion (do we have the leadership pipeline?). For policymakers, the implications are that healthy, inclusive workplaces contribute to economic stability and growth, suggesting that encouraging corporate investments in workforce development (via incentives or regulations) has societal benefits.

In closing, 'The business case for humanity' is no longer just a slogan; it is an evidence-backed reality. Companies that honour the human element by building inclusive, engaging and growth-oriented cultures are building the most valuable asset of all: a motivated, high-performing workforce. This translates directly to stronger innovation, customer satisfaction, and financial returns.

As we've seen, some of the world's best-performing organisations have already embraced this truth. The question is not whether investing in people pays off, but how quickly those who haven't embraced it will catch up. The competitive advantages of the past (scale, capital, patents) are increasingly being overtaken by the competitive advantage of having the best team, culture, and purpose. Ultimately, putting people first is not just an ethical choice; it is one of the wisest business choices a leader can make for long-term success.

Ultimately, every metric – revenue, profit, innovation, market share – stems from people. Trust, empathy, inclusion, and purpose are not soft; they're strategic. The question isn't whether you can afford to prioritise humanity. The real question is: Can you afford not to?

The question isn't whether you can afford to prioritise humanity. The real question is: Can you afford not to?

3

THE REAL COMPETITIVE EDGE

AI isn't only mimicking human intelligence; it's stretching the boundaries of creativity, even in areas steeped in tradition and history. We're no longer asking if AI can create. We're learning from what it creates. This isn't the future; it's happening now. The good thing is, you are less likely to suffer from the AI wave and more likely to benefit from it if you embrace it. The choice is yours.

There is an urgency for individuals, businesses, and educational institutions to proactively adapt to the rapidly changing AI landscape. Emphasising human-centric skills and ethical considerations will be crucial in navigating the challenges and opportunities presented by AI advancements.

For decades, businesses have pursued efficiency with an almost singular focus, measuring success primarily through the lens of productivity and financial returns. Efficiency is seductive, offering tangible, quantifiable results, and swift returns on investment. Yet, as the digital era accelerates and AI advances, a critical question emerges: what value remains uniquely human in an increasingly automated world?

AI as Autonomous Competitors

A recent discussion by Steven Bartlett (Diary of a CEO) and a panel of thought leaders including Daniel Priestley, Amjad Masad, and Bret Weinstein, highlights the transformative impact of AI agents.[1] These are no longer mere tools aiding human productivity; they have evolved into autonomous entities capable of performing sophisticated tasks without human intervention. Within the next two years, roles traditionally viewed as secure, ranging from customer service to programming and content creation, face significant threats of displacement by AI.

This profound shift marks an urgent turning point. Efficiency, once the ultimate competitive edge, now risks becoming the baseline, the minimum standard necessary for survival rather than a unique advantage.

As automation makes efficiency commonplace, competitive advantage increasingly relies on uniquely human qualities like empathy, creativity, emotional intelligence, and ethical reasoning. These qualities form the human advantage, a space where AI, despite its remarkable capabilities, still struggles to fully replicate.

While AI can analyse data and replicate patterns, genuine creativity driven by intuition, insight, and original thought remains distinctly human. Businesses leveraging creativity can unlock innovation and redefine market boundaries in ways purely analytical or efficiency-driven approaches cannot.

Similarly, empathy becomes invaluable in creating connections and delivering personalised experiences. The capacity to deeply understand customer needs, fears, aspirations, and motivation is an irreplaceable human skill that builds lasting relationships and brand loyalty, transcending the transactional nature of automated interactions.

To harness the potential of empathy and creativity, there must be a radical rethinking of educational systems and talent strategies. Current educational models, rooted deeply in the industrial age and designed primarily for efficiency, are ill-equipped for this new reality. Schools and training programmes must pivot towards cultivating adaptability, critical thinking, emotional intelligence and lifelong learning to empower individuals for continuous, dynamic changes in their professional lives.

Organisations must also shift their talent acquisition and development strategies, prioritising potential, creativity, and adaptability over narrow skill sets that AI could soon replicate. Leadership will require a renewed emphasis on coaching, mentorship and creating cultures where creativity and empathy are not just encouraged but strategically cultivated and rewarded.

Ethical Leadership in the AI Era

As AI gains prevalence, ethical considerations also become paramount. Leaders and businesses must maintain vigilance over AI applications, ensuring human oversight to prevent biases and unintended consequences. Empathy and ethical reasoning become not just desirable but essential leadership qualities in ensuring AI serves humanity beneficially and responsibly.

The era of relying solely on efficiency as a competitive edge is rapidly diminishing. In a world where AI handles efficiency, the enduring and distinctly human advantages are empathy and creativity. By embracing these qualities, leaders and organisations can ensure not only relevance but also flourishing in the new competitive landscape shaped by automation. The future belongs not merely to the efficient but profoundly to the empathetic and the creative.

Why Efficiency Is No Longer Enough

Considering the current advancements in AI, where it can analyse massive datasets, streamline logistics and even produce artwork, it is natural to question the role and place of humans in this rapidly changing technological landscape. Examining the unique and irreplaceable characteristics that are fundamentally defining aspects of human intelligence is the solution to this puzzle.

1. **Empathy:** A crucial skill that involves the capacity to forge connections, comprehend others' emotions, and expertly utilise emotional intelligence to lead and inspire.

2. **Creativity:** The remarkable capacity to not only innovate and think divergently but also to push the boundaries of existing data and explore uncharted territories of thought and innovation.

3. **Critical thinking:** A crucial skill involving the interpretation of information, questioning of assumptions and navigation of complex ethical dilemmas represents a cognitive

capacity that currently remains beyond the capabilities of AI.

Efficiency maximises what exists. Creativity and empathy build what's next.

Case Study: Why Google Prioritises Creativity Over Optimisation

Google, despite being a data-driven tech giant, actively fosters creativity and empathy in its leadership and product design. When Google introduced the '20 per cent time' policy, allowing employees to dedicate a fifth of their time to passion projects, the result was groundbreaking innovations, including **Gmail and Google Maps**.[2] Instead of forcing optimisation, Google empowered human ingenuity. The lesson? Efficiency alone won't create the next industry-disrupting idea. Creativity will.

Empathy: The New Leadership Superpower

For a considerable period, the crucial role of empathy within effective leadership has been underestimated and underappreciated. Many mistakenly consider it a "soft skill," a desirable but not essential element of business success – despite its importance. Their assessment of the situation is inaccurate and misleading.

In today's global, AI-driven world, leaders who lead with **empathy drive higher innovation, employee engagement and customer loyalty.**

- The data indicates a significant correlation between manager empathy and employee engagement, with employees reporting 76 per cent higher engagement levels when working under empathetic leadership compared to those under less empathetic leaders.

- In terms of revenue growth, companies that demonstrate high levels of empathy have been shown to outperform their competitors by a significant margin, achieving a 20 per cent increase.

- A recent survey revealed that a significant portion of the workforce – 58 per cent to be exact – indicated a willingness to leave their current position if their supervisors showed a deficiency in empathy and understanding.

Empathy boosts productivity, not through sheer hard work, but by fostering a smarter approach, one that involves a deep understanding of people's motivations, the removal of any obstacles hindering their progress and the cultivation of an environment where talent can truly thrive and flourish.

Culture as Strategy: Top-Rated Case Studies

1. **Bain & Company: A Culture of Connection and Consistency**
   Bain has consistently ranked among the top Glassdoor companies globally. At its core is a culture of trust, mentor-

ship, and psychological comfort and safety. Bain's approach is deeply people-first, prioritising not just high performance but high belonging. Feedback flows both ways, coaching is embedded at every level, and employees consistently note that 'people genuinely care.' This creates a reinforcing cycle of excellence where team members feel seen, valued, and empowered to lead.

2. **NVIDIA: Psychological Safety in a High-Performance Environment**
NVIDIA's culture blends innovation with humanity. Despite being at the cutting edge of AI and graphics technology, employees rank the culture highly because leadership fosters transparency, encourages curiosity, and champions mental well-being. Leaders are known for making space for questions and for respecting the 'how' as much as the 'what' in delivery. Employees report feeling safe to challenge ideas, which directly fuels creativity and risk-taking, critical ingredients for NVIDIA's continued growth.

3. **Eli Lilly: Empathy, Purpose, and Performance in Healthcare**
Eli Lilly has built a values-driven culture rooted in empathy, both internally and externally. The company empowers employees through purpose-driven work, inclusive leadership, and meaningful recognition. Employees speak of being 'treated like humans, not numbers', and of seeing leaders actively

walk the talk. In a sector known for pressure and burnout, Eli Lilly stands out for protecting well-being while delivering exceptional results.

These companies prove that culture is not a nice-to-have; it's a performance strategy. Psychological safety, empathy, and clarity of purpose are not just feel-good ideas. They drive results, engagement, innovation, and retention. In times of change, they become the anchor that keeps people and performance grounded.

Creativity: The Last True Competitive Edge

AI has the capacity not only to generate various forms of content but also to replicate existing artistic styles with impressive accuracy and even to compose original pieces of music. Nevertheless, the following tasks remain beyond its capabilities.

1. While AI excels at processing and repurposing existing data, the ability to generate novel concepts remains a distinctly human skill.

2. The essence of creativity is often found in challenging the status quo, disrupting existing industry structures and forging new paths – a process that thrives on pattern disruption rather than adherence. AI lacks the capacity to do this.

3. Genuine and authentic creativity is intrinsically linked to and cannot be separated from the tapestry of lived experiences, the full spectrum of human emotions, and the inherent struggles

of the human condition.

While AI can be a valuable tool to aid and enhance creativity, it is important to remember that it is ultimately incapable of replacing the ingenuity and originality of human imagination. An example is Hollywood versus AI-generated scripts. While AI has been utilised in creating screenplays, the resulting works often fall short in terms of conveying genuine emotional depth, subtle nuances and truly original storytelling. Although AI possesses the capability to produce formulas, the truly revolutionary and impactful narratives, such as those seen in films like *Black Panther* and *Parasite*, are fundamentally formed and enriched by the unique perspectives, cultural backgrounds and empathetic understanding that only humans can offer.

The Business Case for Creativity

The engine of economic growth is fuelled by the innovative ideas and creative solutions generated by individuals and businesses. Contributing a staggering $2.25 trillion to the global economy, the creative sector plays a significant role in worldwide commerce and economic growth. A 14 per cent higher revenue growth is seen in organisations that place a high value on creativity compared to their competitors who do not prioritise fostering a creative environment. Because creative companies foster innovation, they are better able to attract and retain top talent, as people are drawn to work environments where creativity and innovation flourish.

How Businesses Can Cultivate Creativity

1. **Encourage 'Failure-friendly' Culture**
   Truly innovative and groundbreaking ideas are most likely to flourish and be developed in environments that actively encourage experimentation and do not penalise or discourage risk-taking. Pixar and Netflix actively promote 'candour sessions'. These sessions are designed to encourage employees to openly and constructively challenge ideas in a safe and collaborative environment.

2. **Build Diverse Teams for Stronger Innovation**
   Research shows that teams comprising individuals from diverse backgrounds and experiences generate revenue from innovation that is 19 per cent higher than that of less diverse teams. A remarkable 21 per cent increase in profitability has been observed in companies that prioritise gender diversity within their leadership structures, significantly outperforming those with homogenous leadership teams.[3]

3. **Prioritise Human-Centric Product Development**
   In their design process, companies should prioritise the needs of their users above a singular focus on efficiency. This balanced approach is crucial for long-term success and user satisfaction. Apple has achieved remarkable success in the consumer electronics market by consistently designing products that seamlessly blend functionality with aesthetic appeal, intuitive user interfaces, and an emotionally resonant user ex-

perience. Steve Jobs famously stated, 'Design is not just what it looks like and feels like. Design is how it works.'[4]

Case Study: Airbnb's Rise Through Empathy and Creativity

Upon its launch, the innovative Airbnb platform was initially disregarded by established hotel chains, who viewed its business model as inefficient and unlikely to succeed in the long term. However, Airbnb's core strategy centred on fostering human experiences, facilitating cultural connections and developing innovative methods to cultivate trust between hosts and their travellers. The result? It became a thriving business, generating over $100 billion in revenue. This has fundamentally reshaped and redefined the landscape of the hospitality industry.

Individuals and organisations who can imagine a future that stretches beyond the borders of predictable, streamlined and automated processes are those truly empowered to own the future. This is because the scope of their vision goes beyond past productivity metrics and the allure of optimisation. We achieve groundbreaking results not just by refining existing processes, but by envisioning novel possibilities. The future belongs to those bold enough to look beyond efficiency and ask, '*What else is possible?*'

Key Takeaways

1. **Efficiency optimises; creativity disrupts.** While efficiency refines systems and maximises output, creativity breaks stereotypes and envisages new possibilities. Efficiency sustains; creativity transforms.

2. **AI can automate; empathy connects.** AI is brilliant at handling tasks, analysing data and executing with precision, but trust can only be built by humans who understand nuance and foster genuine connection.

3. **Companies that invest in human skills will outperform those that do not.** In a world powered by technology, only organisations that prioritise emotional intelligence, critical thinking, and collaboration will wield the power to rise and thrive. The future will be dominated, not by the fastest, but by the most human.

In today's world, the competitive edge is no longer solely defined by efficiency. Instead, forward-thinking leaders, companies, and societies are recognising the crucial role of empathy and creativity as fundamental business strategies. Evidently, their future success and dominance are hinged on this pivotal perspective.

The future belongs to those bold enough to look beyond efficiency and ask, 'What else is possible?'

4

LEADING WITH HUMANITY IN THE DIGITAL AGE

The digital age has ushered in a revolution unlike the world has ever seen. From AI to machine learning and automation, technology is reshaping the way we live, work and connect with each other. As a result, businesses are facing an urgent need to adapt to this changing landscape. But there is a crucial question that every leader must answer: how do we balance the power of technology with the intrinsic human needs that are vital to both personal well-being and business success?

In this chapter, we will explore how leaders can navigate this delicate balance and how they can harness the power of technology while ensuring that humanity remains at the core of everything they do. We will delve into practical strategies for leading with empathy, fostering a culture of collaboration, and creating an environment where people thrive in the digital age.

The Impact of Technology on Leadership

In the past few decades, the role of technology in business has shifted dramatically. At one time, leaders primarily relied on intuition, experience, and a few key performance indicators to make decisions. Today, we are awash in data. With the proliferation of digital tools, big data, and analytics, decisions can be made in real time. AI can predict market trends, automate processes and help companies optimise everything from marketing to supply chains. Technology has become the backbone of modern business, enhancing efficiency, productivity, and scalability.

However, while technology has undoubtedly brought about tremendous advancements, it has also introduced new challenges for leaders. In the rush to embrace the latest tools and innovations, companies sometimes lose sight of the human element that is essential for long-term success. The more we embrace automation and digital transformation, the greater the risk of alienating the very people who drive that success: our employees and customers.

Technology Cannot Replace Humanity

No matter how advanced the tools at our disposal become, technology can never replicate the fundamental aspects of being human, which are: empathy, connection, trust, creativity, and emotional intelligence. These are the qualities that enable us to build meaningful relationships, foster innovation, and inspire others. As leaders, our job is to ensure that these human qualities are not only preserved but actively nurtured in an increasingly digital world.

Empathy, for example, is something that technology cannot replace. In fact, it is more important than ever for leaders to lead with empathy. As automation takes over routine tasks, employees are left with a deep need for purpose, connection, and recognition. They want to feel heard, understood, and valued, not just as cogs in the machine, but as people with unique experiences and contributions.

Leaders must recognise that technology can help meet certain human needs. For instance, AI can handle repetitive administrative tasks, freeing up employees to focus on creative, value-driven work. Technology can connect teams across geographical boundaries, allowing for more collaboration and innovation. But it's up to leaders to use technology in a way that enhances the human experience rather than diminishes it.

The Power of Empathetic Leadership in the Digital Age

Empathetic leadership is about understanding the needs of others, whether it's employees, customers, or partners, and responding in a way that reflects care and concern. In a digital age, where automation often leads to a sense of detachment, empathetic leadership is a critical differentiator. But what does it look like in practice?

1. **Listening Actively**

    Empathetic leaders listen to their teams. They take time to understand the challenges their employees face and the aspirations they hold. In an age where digital communication has made us more connected than ever, it's also made us more distanced. Leaders who listen actively break down those barriers and create a space for authentic communication.

2. **Building Trust**

Trust is the foundation of any effective relationship, which is crucial in the digital age. With the rise of surveillance technologies and the widespread use of data, employees may feel like they're being monitored more than supported. Leaders need to build trust by being transparent about how they use technology, especially when it comes to personal data. They should also lead by example, demonstrating honesty, vulnerability, and integrity in their own actions.

3. **Recognising Human Effort**

In a world where automation can perform tasks faster and more efficiently than any human, leaders must make an intentional effort to recognise the unique value that people bring to the table. Celebrating human creativity, problem-solving and emotional intelligence helps reinforce the idea that people are the true engines of innovation, even in a tech-driven world.

4. **Providing Support for Well-Being**

The rapid pace of technological advancement can sometimes leave employees feeling overwhelmed or disconnected. Leaders have a responsibility to prioritise the well-being of their teams, creating environments that take mental and emotional health seriously. This means promoting work-life balance, offering mental health resources and encouraging a culture where people feel safe expressing concerns without fear of judgement or retribution.

Creating a Culture of Collaboration in the Digital Era

While technology has the potential to foster greater collaboration across teams and geographies, it's still up to leaders to create a culture that encourages true collaboration. Many organisations often use digital tools in silos, with different departments or teams relying on their own systems, creating barriers to communication and cooperation.

This challenge can be overcome by promoting cross-functional collaboration, which encourages employees from different departments to work together, share knowledge and innovate across organisational boundaries. Tools like video conferencing, project management platforms, and collaborative workspaces can help bridge gaps, but it's up to leaders to create an environment that values collective problem-solving.

A case study that comes to mind is McDonald's launching All Day Breakfast (ADB) through cross-functional collaboration.[1]

McDonald's 2015 All Day Breakfast launch succeeded because of strong cross-departmental collaboration. Marketing generated buzz via social media; the supply chain ensured all-day breakfast. The kitchen updated workflows for the new menu. Digital tools enabled quick team decisions. Teamwork made ADB's nationwide launch successful.

1. **Emphasising Purpose-Driven Work**
   Technology alone isn't enough to motivate employees. People want to feel that their work has meaning. Leaders should align their teams around a shared purpose that goes beyond profit margins and production metrics. By focusing on the positive impact of their work, whether that's improving customer experiences, advancing social causes or solving enormous problems, leaders can create a sense of belonging and motivation that technology alone cannot provide.

2. **Fostering Inclusivity**
   Technology has the power to democratise access to information and resources, but it's up to leaders to ensure that all employees, regardless of their background or role, have an equal opportunity to contribute. A culture of inclusion is essential for leveraging the full potential of a diverse workforce, and technology can be a powerful enabler when used in the right way.

The Future: A Human-Tech Partnership

The digital age is not about choosing between technology and humanity; it's about finding ways for both to coexist and complement one another. The best leaders of the future will be those who understand that technology can be a powerful tool to enhance human potential, not a replacement for it.

In the coming years, we will see a shift from a 'man versus machine' mentality to a more integrated approach, where technology and human qualities work hand-in-hand. This is the true essence of the human advantage in the digital age: harnessing the power of technology to amplify human connection, creativity, and empathy, while never losing sight of the values that make us human.

As leaders, we must guide our organisations through this transition, ensuring that as we embrace innovation, we also safeguard the values and practices that nurture our humanity. When technology is wielded with empathy, creativity, and purpose, the result is a more resilient, innovative, and human-centred organisation, one where technology amplifies human potential, rather than diminishing it.

Case Study: IBM Watson in Healthcare

To improve diagnostic speed and accuracy, particularly in cancer, IBM Watson's advanced analytical capabilities have been integrated into a range of healthcare institutions to provide crucial support to medical professionals. Watson leverages its ability to analyse structured and unstructured data on a massive scale to generate treatment recommendations supported by concrete evidence. This process enhances but does not replace the crucial role of human expertise in healthcare.[2]

Case Study: Airbus and AI-assisted Aircraft Design

In a collaborative effort with human engineers, Airbus has successfully utilised cutting-edge generative design technology, driven by AI, to produce aircraft components that are both significantly lighter and more energy-efficient.[3] This process serves as a prime example of the powerful synergy that can be achieved when the capabilities of machines are combined with the ingenuity and creativity of humans, resulting in a truly collaborative and innovative outcome.

Case Study: Lily Hospital, Warri, Delta State, Nigeria

In the heart of Nigeria's Niger Delta region, Lily Hospital in Warri has established itself as a beacon of quality healthcare and leadership. Founded in 1984, the hospital has grown steadily to become one of the region's most trusted private medical institutions. Now, it is entering a pivotal phase – embracing a human-tech partnership to shape the future of healthcare delivery, not just within its walls, but across the wider ecosystem.

Unlike many digital transformation journeys that start with technology adoption, Lily Hospital's approach has been grounded in strengthening human capacity first. The hospital has focused on clinical excellence, operational discipline, and patient trust, laying the groundwork for responsible and context-sensitive technology integration.

Recognising that the future of healthcare lies in smart augmentation, Lily Hospital is preparing to roll out AI tools to accelerate diagnostics and data analytics. From radiology to patient trend forecasting, these tools will be used not as replacements for clinicians, but as enablers, supporting faster, more accurate decision-making and freeing up human time for empathy-driven care.

The Launch of Lily Hospital Academy

One of the most transformative investments is *Lily Academy* – a visionary initiative that signals the hospital's long-term commitment to human development. The academy will serve multiple functions such as:

- Training the next generation of healthcare workers, helping to address the acute talent gap in Nigeria and the region.

- Building leadership and management capability within the healthcare sector.

- Serving as a centre for research and innovation, particularly on the intersection of digital health, community care, and system design.

By investing in education and research, Lily Hospital is not just using technology; it is actively shaping the future workforce that will partner with it.

A Thoughtful Tech Transition

Rather than rushing into digital adoption, Lily Hospital is taking a **deliberate, human-led approach**. It is designing workflows that prioritise clinician input, patient experience, and ethical deployment of technology. Staff are being prepared to work alongside AI in ways that enhance, not erode the relational aspect of care.

This forward-looking approach is especially important in a context where digital infrastructure and health equity remain uneven. By embedding inclusion, learning, and leadership development into its transformation journey, Lily Hospital offers a model for sustainable innovation in emerging markets.

A Vision for Scalable Impact

Lily Hospital's strategy illustrates that the human-tech partnership is not just about tools; it's about mindset, readiness, and trust. As it prepares to fully integrate AI and digital systems, it does so with clarity of purpose: to amplify the human touch in healthcare, to grow future leaders, and to build a system where innovation and inclusion go hand in hand.

Case Study: Informa plc

In 2020, as the COVID-19 pandemic swept across the globe, organisations faced a pivotal test of values. The crisis was not just a health emergency; it was a leadership challenge, demanding swift decisions under pressure, and compassion amid chaos. For Informa plc, a global events, publishing, and business intelligence company, the response became a defining moment in human-centred leadership.

The Challenge: Leading Through Disruption

As in-person events were cancelled globally and revenues took an immediate hit, Informa was confronted with the very real pressures of operational disruption, financial instability, and workforce anxiety. With a global footprint spanning over 30 countries and thousands of employees, the temptation to prioritise commercial survival over employee well-being was real.

But Informa chose a different path. Under the direction of senior leadership and its Group CEO, Lord Stephen A. Carter, Informa made a bold, values-driven decision: to put people first, no matter the cost. Key actions included:

- **Job security and support:** Rather than widespread layoffs, Informa launched a 'Colleague Support Fund', which provided financial assistance to staff facing exceptional hardship. Senior leaders took voluntary pay reductions to protect jobs across the business.

- **Flexible working as a policy, not a perk:** Informa quickly adapted to hybrid and remote working models, introducing flexibility as a long-term approach. Well-being days and meeting-free zones were encouraged to combat virtual fatigue and support mental health.

- **Zoom-free Fridays:** One of the most praised initiatives was the introduction of 'Zoom-free Fridays'. Leaders recognised the toll that constant video calls were having on morale and acted decisively to protect space for uninterrupted work and personal renewal.

- **Human-led communication:** Frequent, transparent updates from leadership created psychological safety and psychological comfort. Leadership treated colleagues as partners in navigating uncertainty, instead of imposing radio silence or top-down policies.

While many organisations struggled with mass resignations and disengagement, Informa deepened trust. Engagement scores remained strong, and the business emerged more agile, inclusive, and resilient. In the years since, many of the well-being and flexible work policies introduced during the pandemic have been retained and have evolved.

One of the senior leaders had this to say: 'We didn't get everything right – but we never stopped asking, "What do our people need most right now?" That one question shaped every decision we made.'

Informa's pandemic response was more than crisis management. It was a demonstration of **the human advantage** in practice – leading with empathy, transparency, and trust. It proved that when people feel seen, supported, and safe, performance doesn't just survive – it transforms.

In a world increasingly driven by AI, algorithms, and automation, this case study is a reminder that *humanity*, not just technology, will determine which businesses thrive.

Empathy, resilience, adaptability, and purpose aren't soft skills; they're strategic assets.

5

The Future of Leadership

As we hurtle towards a future defined by AI, automation, and technological transformation, it's easy to assume that leadership will be driven by data, algorithms, and machine learning. After all, machines can analyse vast amounts of information, predict market trends, and even automate decision-making. But despite the growing influence of technology, there is one thing that machines will never replicate: the human experience. This is a crucial insight for the leaders of tomorrow.

The future of leadership will hinge, not on a leader's ability to master spreadsheets or complex algorithms, but on their ability to connect, inspire, and engage with people. As technology continues to evolve, the human skills leaders need to thrive are becoming more critical than ever. These skills are the foundation of emotional intelligence, empathy, creativity, and resilience – traits that cannot be automated, replicated or outsourced.

In this chapter, we explore the human skills that will define effective leadership in the future, and why these skills are not just nice-to-have but are essential for long-term success. We'll also look at global examples of companies and leaders who are already embracing these principles and leading the charge in a world where the human advantage is the ultimate differentiator.

The Rise of Human-Centric Leadership

For centuries, authority, hierarchy, and control have defined leadership. But in the 21st century, the landscape of leadership is shifting. Leaders no longer command from the top down but lead from within their teams, fostering collaboration, engagement, and shared ownership. This shift has been accelerated by the digital revolution and the rise of remote working, where flexibility, trust, and emotional connection have become paramount.

In 2023, a global survey conducted by Deloitte found that 88 per cent of business leaders believe that 'creating a culture of inclusion and belonging' will be key to their success over the next five years.[1] The report also highlighted that 'empathy' was rated as the most critical leadership trait for the future. This isn't just about being nice; it's about creating environments where people feel heard, valued, and connected to the company's purpose.

So, what are the human skills that leaders need to master in the coming years? Let's break them down:

1. **Resilience: Bouncing Back in a World of Uncertainty**
   The future is uncertain, and the ability to handle setbacks and navigate challenges will be a hallmark of great leaders. Resilience is about more than just enduring difficult times;

it's about adapting, learning, and growing from adversity. Jacinda Ardern, former Prime Minister of New Zealand, exemplified resilience during her leadership, particularly in the aftermath of the Christchurch Mosque shootings in 2019 and the COVID-19 pandemic.[2] Her empathetic leadership, calmness under pressure and ability to unite the country through crises became a global example of how to lead with strength and compassion. Her leadership was a testament to the fact that resilience doesn't mean merely 'toughing it out' but also showing vulnerability, authenticity, and care for others during times of crisis.

The ability to stay grounded and focused, despite external pressures, will be essential for leaders as they navigate a world of constant change, from geopolitical uncertainties to economic volatility and the ongoing impact of climate change.

2. **Adaptability: Leading Through Change**
Adaptability is arguably one of the most important skills for future leaders. With the rapid pace of technological advancements, leaders need to not only be comfortable with change but also actively drive it. The rise of automation, AI, and digital transformation means that roles, skill sets, and even entire industries are being reshaped before our eyes.

One remarkable example of adaptability is Indra Nooyi, former CEO of PepsiCo. Nooyi transformed PepsiCo during her tenure by embracing healthier products and focusing on sustainability. She foresaw the shifting tides of consumer preferences and led the company through a significant strategic overhaul, positioning PepsiCo as a leader in healthier snack and beverage options.[3]

As industries continue to evolve, leaders must possess the ability to pivot quickly, anticipate future trends, and steer their organisations through periods of disruption. The world's most successful leaders will be those who are not rigid in their thinking but are open to experimentation, learning, and adapting in real-time.

3. **Creativity and Innovation: Fostering an Environment for New Ideas**
While creativity has traditionally been associated with the arts, in the digital age, it's a vital leadership skill. As technology automates more routine tasks, human creativity becomes the differentiating factor. Leaders who can inspire creativity, cultivate innovative thinking, and push the boundaries of what's possible will be the ones who succeed.

Consider Elon Musk, CEO of Tesla and SpaceX, who has built his companies on a foundation of groundbreaking innovation. Whether it's the development of electric vehicles, reusable rockets, or ambitious plans for colonising Mars, Musk has shown how embracing creativity and a willingness to take risks can transform entire industries. Though his leadership style divides opinion, it highlights how disruptive vision can drive technological shifts.

The most successful leaders of the future will be those who can unlock their teams' creative potential, create a culture where new ideas are welcomed, and transform those ideas into tangible results.

4. **Purpose-Driven Leadership**

Purpose-driven leadership will define the future. The younger generations, particularly Millennials and Gen Z, increasingly want to work for organisations that align with their values. They want to know that their work has a broader impact and contributes to something meaningful. Patagonia, the outdoor clothing brand, provides an inspiring example. The company's commitment to environmental sustainability and ethical business practices has helped it build a loyal customer base and create a thriving culture of employees who are passionate about the company's mission. Their bold stance on environmental issues, including pledging to donate 1 per cent of sales to environmental causes, has made them a leader not only in business but also in advocacy for social and environmental change.[4]

Leaders who can authentically align their company's vision with their own values and the values of their teams will inspire deeper engagement and long-term loyalty. Purpose-driven leadership isn't a passing trend; it's the future.

5. **Empathetic Leadership: Leading with Humanity**
In the digital age's whirlwind of technological change, a new breed of leaders is proving that 'human-centred' skills, such as empathy, adaptability, resilience, creativity, and purpose, are the key to lasting success. Purpose drives performance even amid rapid tech transformation.

During multiple crises – the 2019 Christchurch Mosque shootings, the COVID-19 pandemic and a volcanic eruption, Ardern combined empathy and resilience to unite her country. After the Christchurch attack, the image of Ardern hugging a Muslim survivor, clad in a headscarf, became an international symbol of compassionate leadership. Her 'complete embrace' of the Islamic community showcased strength and kindness that transformed what it means to be a leader globally.

In the pandemic, Ardern chose an 'empathetic approach' of front-facing communication and inclusivity, including candid Facebook Live chats from her home, which built public trust. The result was extraordinary: 92 per cent of New Zealanders were satisfied with the government's handling of COVID-19, one of the highest approval rates in the world for a pandemic response.[5]

Ardern's leadership was also highly adaptive and data-driven. She 'brought in data, engaged experts and worked collaboratively' across party lines. Notably, during a cattle disease outbreak called Mycoplasma bovis, she convened agricultural leaders and, through a cooperative process, arrived at a consensus to eradicate the disease – a bold plan now on track in a 10-year programme.

Throughout each challenge, Ardern asked, 'How do we remember the human experience in all of this?' This philosophy led her to prioritise compassion and common humanity in policymaking. For example, she introduced a national well-being budget focusing on poverty reduction and mental health, aligning economic policies with human outcomes. Such moves, alongside her vulnerable honesty about struggles like imposter syndrome, showcased authenticity and emotional intelligence.

Ardern's tenure showed that empathy and decisiveness are not mutually exclusive. In fact, embracing empathy made her a 'more well-rounded problem solver'. New Zealand's low COVID death rate and cohesive societal response as well as Ardern's sky-high domestic and international esteem (she topped trust and approval polls) validate the power of empathetic, adaptive governance for long-term societal resilience.

Case Study: Tony Elumelu (Nigeria)

Tony O. Elumelu exemplifies purpose-driven leadership, championing 'Africapitalism', – the belief that Africa's private sector should drive development through long-term investment in people.

The Tony Elumelu Foundation annually gives $5,000 to 1,000 African entrepreneurs. $100M in 2015 fuelled startup job creation and economic growth.[6] Elumelu believes leadership is about elevating others: 'My success is also about the success of others,' he says, emphasising talent development and creating pathways for human capital to thrive. This empathetic approach has built loyal teams and a wide network of protégés.

Elumelu's vision transformed a failing Nigerian bank into the Pan-African United Bank for Africa (UBA), operating in over 20 countries.[7] His leadership blends ethical discipline with empowerment, urging leaders to 'find in people what they didn't know they had'. By aligning profit with purpose, he has delivered strong business performance through UBA, Transcorp, and Heirs Holdings, while fostering widespread impact. Named among the Time100 Most Influential People in 2020, Elumelu is recognised for fuelling entrepreneurship that has created over 400,000 jobs. His story proves that compassionate, people-focused leadership can drive inclusive growth and market success.[8]

Case Study: Audrey Tang (Taiwan)

Audrey Tang, Taiwan's Digital Minister turned 'Digital Ambassador', practises a human-centred approach to technology and governance.[9] A former civic hacker, Tang promotes open, collaborative democracy using digital tools to build empathy and consensus. Her Taiwan platform invites citizens, experts, and officials to debate policy online. Using Pol.is software and AI, it surfaces broad agreement rather than amplifying loud voices. In one case, polarised views on Uber converged around a shared concern for rider safety, leading to practical regulations. This radically inclusive model has informed dozens of laws with minimal partisanship, reflecting Tang's belief in 'remembering the human element' in tech and using AI to foster understanding.

Tang's leadership also emphasises adaptability and transparency. During COVID-19, she helped launch a publicly developed mask distribution app, earning public trust through openness and responsiveness.[10] Her 'radical transparency' approach includes weekly questions and answers (Q&As) and publishing government code, contributing to Taiwan's globally admired pandemic response.

Tang's consensus-driven, human-first model is now studied internationally, highlighting that true digital transformation isn't just technological; it's about making institutions more empathetic, collaborative, and responsive. Her work shows how tech can be a bridge between people, reshaping governance for the digital age.

Case Study: Semco (Brazil)

In South America, Semco, a Brazilian manufacturer, offers a striking example of human-centred leadership under maverick CEO Ricardo Semler.[11] Semco embraced 'radical democracy' in the workplace, with employees participating in key decisions, voting on manager salaries and having a say in company investments. Instead of rigid rules, the company relied on trust, flexibility and long-term well-being. Workers designed their own schedules and workspaces, creating a culture of empowerment and ownership. This approach fostered deep engagement and adaptability. During economic downturns, employees agreed to shared sacrifices like pay cuts or role-shifts, avoiding layoffs and later sharing in the profits.

Semco's results were remarkable: over two decades, revenue grew from $4 million to $200 million despite economic instability. The company's low turnover and high job applicant rates showed that its people-first culture was a clear advantage. Even after Semler's departure in the late 2000s, Semco's model continues to influence global firms seeking innovation through empowerment. In today's Digital Era, Semco proves that treating employees as trusted partners can build resilient, creative, and loyal teams that drive lasting success.

Case Study: Patagonia (USA)

Few companies embody purpose-driven leadership like Patagonia. Under founder Yvon Chouinard and CEO Ryan Gellert, the company has prioritised both people and the planet through employee-friendly policies and bold environmental activism. Patagonia empowers workers with flexibility, on-site childcare, and time for personal passions like surfing or volunteering. This trust-driven culture fosters innovation and loyalty, contributing to low turnover and long-term success. Even during digital disruption, Patagonia stayed true to its values, focusing on quality, ethical supply chains, and environmental repairability over fast fashion. This authenticity has fuelled strong sales and customer loyalty.

In 2022, Chouinard made headlines by transferring 98 per cent of Patagonia's $3 billion equity to a non-profit trust, ensuring all future profits go to fighting climate change.[12] This bold act capped years of purpose-led decisions, including donating 1 per cent of sales to environmental causes and running the iconic 'Don't Buy This Jacket' ad. Far from hurting business, these actions quadrupled Patagonia's revenue from 2005 to 2020 and earned it a reputation as one of the world's most ethical brands. Patagonia shows that combining empathy with environmental purpose can yield enduring commercial and societal value.

These cases – from tech and government to business and activism, show that the human side of leadership is a decisive edge in the digital age. Empathy, resilience, adaptability, and purpose aren't soft skills; they're strategic assets. Leaders like Chouinard, Elumelu, Tang, and Semler prove that putting people and principles first builds trust, drives innovation and ensures long-term impact. As AI and remote work reshape the world, human-centred leadership is not just relevant; it's essential to future success.

The future of leadership will hinge, not on a leader's ability to master spreadsheets or complex algorithms, but on their ability to connect, inspire, and engage with people.

6

Emotional Intelligence

The 21st-century workplace is no longer powered by control and compliance; it thrives on connection, trust, and psychological safety. At the heart of this transformation lies emotional intelligence, a leadership superpower that helps unlock not only performance but also purpose, creativity, and resilience.

In a fast-changing world shaped by hybrid work, generational shifts, and global disruption, emotional intelligence is no longer optional. It is the ultimate leadership skill that enables all others.

This chapter explores how emotionally intelligent leaders create environments where people don't just work; they *flourish*.

What Emotional Intelligence Is

Coined by psychologists Peter Salovey and John D. Mayer and popularised by Daniel Goleman, emotional intelligence is the capacity to recognise, understand, manage, and influence emotions; ours and those of others.[1]

Goleman breaks EQ into five domains:
1. Self-awareness

2. Self-regulation

3. Motivation

4. Empathy

5. Social skills

These are not 'soft' skills; they are core competencies for effective leadership in complex, human-centred systems.

Why EQ Matters More Than Ever

According to a study by McKinsey, the demand for social and emotional skills in the workplace will grow by 26 per cent by 2030. EQ is now strongly correlated with business success, team engagement, and retention.[2]

In high-EQ environments:[3]

- Employees are four times more likely to feel engaged.

- Teams report 40 per cent higher trust levels.

- Turnover decreases by up to 30 per cent.

In low-EQ environments:

- Toxic cultures flourish

- Innovation stagnates

- Silent attrition increases (quiet quitters)

Put simply, emotionally intelligent leadership isn't a luxury; it's a performance imperative.

Case Studies in Emotional Intelligence: Leading with Heart, not Hierarchy

Emotional intelligence isn't confined to boardrooms or leadership retreats; it lives in the decisions leaders make when no one is watching, in how they show up for people, especially those often overlooked. Here are two extraordinary but often underappreciated examples of EQ in action:

Case Study: Hamdi Ulukaya – Compassion as a Corporate Strategy

When Hamdi Ulukaya, a Kurdish-Turkish immigrant, founded Chobani, he didn't set out to create just a yoghurt company; he set out to build a different kind of business – one where people, especially those most vulnerable, came first.

At a time when many leaders measure success by profit margins alone, Ulukaya embedded emotional intelligence into the fabric of his company. He hired refugees and immigrants from over 20 countries, turning Chobani's production floors into multicultural ecosystems where inclusion wasn't a strategy; it was survival. Across his plants, workers speak over 30 languages, but their shared cultural value is dignity.[4]

In 2016, Ulukaya made headlines by giving 10 per cent of his company's shares to employees.[5] He also introduced six-week paid parental leave for all staff, full-time and hourly, a rarity in manufacturing. His emotional awareness of the lived experiences of his workers, many of whom came from unstable regions or held marginalised identities – informed decisions that combined business acumen with empathy.

The outcome? Chobani became the top-selling Greek yoghurt brand in the U.S., and a case study in how purpose and profit cannot only coexist but fuel each other.

Ulukaya's leadership exemplifies empathy, social awareness, and authentic connection – key EQ domains that transformed an everyday product into a movement powered by people.

Case Study: Dr Kakenya Ntaiya – Emotional Intelligence as Cultural Courage

'I wanted to change the tradition. But first, I had to live through it.'—Dr Kakenya Ntaiya.[6]

Born in rural Kenya, Dr Kakenya Ntaiya was engaged at five and expected to undergo female genital mutilation (FGM) as a teenager, a deeply entrenched rite of passage in her community. She made a pact with her father: she would undergo the ritual if he allowed her to finish school. That decision altered the trajectory of her life.

Kakenya went on to earn a PhD, and instead of leaving her past behind, she returned home to change the future. She founded the

Kakenya Centre for Excellence, a school that offers girls a haven from FGM and early marriage, and a pathway to education, leadership, and agency.

What makes her leadership extraordinary isn't just what she built; it's how she did it. Kakenya works hand-in-hand with village elders, parents, and even local boys, engaging them in open, respectful dialogue. She didn't try to dismantle her culture with blame or shame. She understood its emotional roots – the fear, the pride, the silence – and led change from within.

Her emotional intelligence, her empathy, cultural sensitivity, and ability to build trust, became her greatest tools. She modelled what it means to honour your heritage while refusing to be confined by it.

Her story resonates deeply with my life. I was the only child in my family to refuse FGM – a decision that, like Kakenya's, came with consequences. This was more than rejecting a ritual. It was a rebellion against centuries of power structures – a quiet revolution against pain cloaked in tradition.

Defying FGM meant risking isolation, carrying shame, and confronting the belief that choosing differently meant I no longer belonged. But I knew then what I still believe now: change never comes from silence. It comes from the courage to be the first.

That single act of refusal wasn't just about protecting myself. It was about breaking a generational cycle for my daughters, nieces, and granddaughters. I chose not to inherit pain, and I chose not to pass it down.

Kakenya's journey and mine show that emotional intelligence is not just about managing emotions. It's about understanding systems, feeling the weight of history, and still choosing to lead with empathy. It's proof that culture can evolve, and leadership can heal.

Today, over **500 girls** have passed through the Kakenya Centre, and many have become changemakers themselves. Like so many untold stories across the world, hers reminds us that the most transformative leadership often begins not in positions of power, but in moments of personal defiance, led not by fear, but by vision.

Why These Stories Matter

These aren't typical corporate case studies. They're reminders that emotionally intelligent leadership isn't defined by role or title; it's defined by how we treat others, especially when it's inconvenient. Whether in a boardroom or a rural village, EQ is the force that humanises leadership and powers lasting change.

As we move further into an era shaped by automation, uncertainty, and polarisation, the question is no longer 'Do you have emotional intelligence?' but 'Do the people around you feel the impact of it?'

EQ in the Workplace: From Awareness to Action

Emotional intelligence begins with self-awareness – the ability to recognise your emotional triggers, biases, and blind spots. This understanding is foundational for personal growth and effective leadership. A practical strategy to build self-awareness is to encourage employees to journal moments of emotional tension and reflect on recurring patterns; after all, awareness precedes transformation. From this base, self-regulation becomes possible. Emotionally intelligent leaders don't suppress emotions – they manage them skilfully. In moments of conflict, using the "pause, breathe, respond" technique creates space for thoughtful decision-making.

Empathy, another core component, is not about fixing but about feeling with others – it's a leadership muscle that strengthens with consistent use. Equally important are motivation and resilience – qualities fuelled by intrinsic drivers rather than external rewards like bonuses or titles. Emotionally intelligent leaders draw from their core values to stay motivated, bounce back from setbacks, and uplift those around them. A practical way to nurture this is by regularly linking tasks and goals to shared values and a long-term sense of purpose, reinforcing internal motivation over external pressure.

Building Emotionally Intelligent Cultures

It's not enough for individual leaders to have high EQ. Organisations must embed emotional intelligence into their DNA through culture, systems, and development.

1. **Training EQ like any other skill:** Programmes that develop self-awareness, active listening and empathy yield measurable business impact. An example is Google's *Search Inside Yourself* programme. It was rooted in mindfulness and emotional intelligence and saw improvements in focus, resilience, and collaboration across teams.[7]

2. **Embedding EQ in hiring and promotion:** Stop hiring only

for IQ and experience. Start prioritising emotional competence, especially for people managers. Use behavioural interview questions, such as 'Tell me about a time you resolved a conflict. What did you learn about yourself?'

3. **Rewarding emotional leadership:** Recognise and celebrate leaders who build trust, show empathy, and model emotional discipline, not just those who hit targets. At Unilever, team health and trust are part of leadership KPIs, reinforcing the value of EQ alongside business results.[8]

Emotional Quotient and Psychological Safety

Amy Edmondson of Harvard Business School defines psychological safety as 'a shared belief that the team is safe for interpersonal risk-taking'.[9] Emotional intelligence is the gateway to building such cultures. Leaders who practise EQ:

- Normalise vulnerability

- Encourage open feedback

- Respond without defensiveness

- Create space for difference

Case Study: Airbnb's Culture of Belonging

Airbnb places emotional intelligence at the core of its leadership model. During the pandemic, CEO Brian Chesky communicated layoffs with transparency, empathy, and dignity. The response from employees and the public was overwhelmingly positive, and Airbnb's brand emerged stronger.[10]

Emotional Quotient Across Cultures

Emotional intelligence is universal, but it manifests differently across cultural contexts. High-EQ leaders practise cultural empathy, adjusting their approach to meet diverse emotional norms.

In Japan, emotional restraint is often valued. In Brazil, emotional expressiveness is more culturally accepted. Leaders with high EQ read these cues and adapt their tone, style, and feedback accordingly. A practical tip before global team interaction is to ask: 'What emotional norms exist in this culture?' Then, lead with curiosity and humility.

Cultivating EQ for Performance, People, and Progress

Emotional intelligence is no longer an optional 'soft skill' in organisations; it has become a core competence that underlies high performance, especially in the context of diverse and dynamic workplaces. The experiences of companies across Asia, Africa, Europe, Latin America, and the Middle East all echo a common theme: when organisations embed EQ into their systems and culture, they unlock greater psychological safety, resilience, innovation, and inclusion. Leaders who lead with emotional intelligence create teams that feel safe and motivated, and these teams produce extraordinary results.

Practical strategies for cultivating EQ at scale include structured coaching programmes, on-the-job exercises that reinforce EQ skills and experiential workshops. Organisations are updating performance management to evaluate *how* results are achieved, rewarding managers who inspire trust and collaboration. Many have made empathy and listening staples of their leadership playbook, and they celebrate culturally intelligent leadership to bridge differences.

Crucially, companies are realising that they must continuously nurture EQ. It's reinforced through hiring (selecting for humility and interpersonal skills), through training and coaching and through leaders exemplifying vulnerability and care in everyday interactions.

In the final analysis, embedding emotional intelligence in an organisation's culture isn't just about 'being nice'; it's about creating the conditions for people to do their best work. When people feel understood and valued, they reciprocate with commitment and creativity. When leaders manage their emotions and respond thoughtfully, they navigate complexity and change with steadiness, modelling resilience for others. And when an entire organisation embraces EQ, it develops a collective resilience and agility, a secret sauce behind long-term sustainable success.

As the cases in this chapter demonstrate, emotional intelligence has moved from the periphery to the centre of effective organisational practice worldwide. Companies that cultivate EQ and integrate it into coaching, teams, performance systems, and values build not just a warmer workplace, but a stronger, more innovative one for the 21st-century global economy.

Change never comes from silence. It comes from the courage to be the first.

7

THE GLOBAL POWER OF INCLUSION

I remember standing in front of a group of about 30 senior leaders where I had been invited to present on a DEI-related topic. These were influential individuals, decision-makers shaping culture, strategy, and the experiences of thousands of people across continents.

Just as I was about to begin the session, one leader spoke up abruptly, voicing their disinterest – almost disdain for DEI. The room fell into a heavy, awkward silence. I could feel the discomfort ripple across the room. In that moment, I felt my legs wobble, my shoulders drop and disappointed – not just by the comment, but by the audacity and visible lack of emotional intelligence and cultural intelligence from someone in such a critical leadership position.

Still, I responded with grace. No animosity. No judgement. No defensiveness. It took a lot of grace because, in all honesty, I was livid internally. I usually don't swear, but in my head that day was an explosion of all kinds of swear words – a stark contrast to my personal values. And yet, I reminded myself of something I've learnt over the years: not every reaction is about us. People bring their wounds, baggage, and fears of being wrong or replaced. They bring their ego. Yes, ego, especially when bruised, can show up as defensiveness, anger, or even hostility. And in moments like that, we have a choice: escalate the tension or create a teachable moment, a space for learning and growth opportunity.

I chose not to be a client to their behaviour by responding in kind. Instead, I chose to lead with humanity and humility. At that moment, I chose kindness over judgement, curiosity over ego. Years of working across cultures and with people from all walks of life have taught me this: when discomfort surfaces, grace is a gift we can offer. I've learnt to create space for vulnerability, to meet resistance with reassurance and to respond to fear with empathy. Not because it's easy, but because it's necessary. Inclusion isn't about being right; it's about being human, especially when it's hard.

I asked the leader to hold their thought; I promised we'd revisit it later and calmly carried on with the session. During the break, they approached me and apologised genuinely. I wasn't hurt at all, so I told them there was no need to apologise to me. Gently, I encouraged them to consider how their words might have landed on others in the room. I explained that if someone present lived with an invisible disability, for example, their remark could have left them feeling unseen, unsafe and unheard. When giving feedback, remember that intent does not erase impact.

The individual returned to the group and offered a heartfelt apology. It was powerful, raw, real, and received with grace by all. Today, that same individual is a trusted ally and a valued friend in my world of work. With their blessing and permission, I share this story.

Here's what I've learnt: We always have the power to choose how we show up and how we choose to use our voice. It is in these defining moments, when discomfort meets dignity and when challenge meets curiosity, that true inclusion takes its root. And that is where growth begins, not just for individuals, but for the people and cultures we lead.

Belonging: The Quiet Force Behind Bold Futures

I have always believed that the true measure of a great organisation is not found in its balance sheets or in its boardrooms. It is not in grand strategy meetings or innovation labs but in the quiet moments when people feel heard, seen, safe and valued for who they are. The true measure of a great organisation is in moments when someone feels safe enough to say, 'I've got an idea' and they're listened to.

In my work across regions and sectors, I've witnessed a powerful truth unfold again and again: when people feel they belong, they stop performing and start *becoming*. They don't just show up; they show up with *fire*. They speak up, they lean in and they stay long enough to help build something better. They share their boldest ideas, take brave, informed or calculated risks and build with others, not just for a pay cheque, but from a place of purpose.

Let's be honest, when people feel excluded, they find creative ways to disengage too, usually right around performance review season.

Inclusion, then, is not a buzzword or a checkbox. It is a leadership choice; a daily decision to create cultures where difference is not just accepted but expected and where voice is not earned through proximity to power but honoured through proximity to truth.

Inclusion, for me, isn't a project or a policy. It's a way of seeing; a leadership mindset that says, 'You matter here – just as you are.' It's also not always comfortable. Inclusion invites challenge. It asks us to re-examine what we've normalised, to get honest about whose voices we prioritise and to stretch beyond the familiar echo chambers we all slip into. (We've all been in those meetings where everyone agrees too quickly. Spoiler: someone's faking it.)

We often talk about innovation, agility, and disruption. But the engine behind those aspirations is human. It's the courage to connect across cultures, the humility to listen, and the wisdom to know that no one builds anything meaningful, alone and in isolation.

Inclusion, belonging and cultural intelligence are not soft ideals; they are *strategic assets*. In a world that is more complex, more connected, and more diverse than ever, they are also non-negotiable. This chapter explores how organisations around the world are reimagining leadership through the lens of humanity. We will be looking at the real power of inclusion, belonging and cultural intelligence, not as HR jargon, but as fuel for innovation, growth, and human brilliance. Not because it's fashionable, but because it's the future.

The Advantage Within

Across every industry and continent, one truth is becoming undeniable: the organisations that will lead the future are those that are inclusive, culturally intelligent and deeply human-centred.

Inclusion is no longer just a moral imperative; it's a strategic business imperative. From fast-growth start-ups to multinational giants, research consistently shows that diverse and inclusive teams outperform their less inclusive counterparts. But it's not diversity alone that drives performance. It's what happens *after* diversity walks through the door, when people feel seen, heard and valued, when psychological safety, cultural intelligence (CQ) and a sense of **belonging** are intentionally cultivated.

This chapter explores the transformative power of inclusion, belonging and CQ. Through global case studies – from Kenya to Japan, Brazil to the United Arab Emirates (UAE) – we'll uncover how organisations are building cultures where difference fuels innovation and how leaders can create environments where everyone thrives.

From Representation to Belonging: Why Inclusion Matters

Representation matters, but without inclusion, it is just optics. And inclusion without belonging is unsustainable. The most effective organisations today go beyond hiring for diversity; they build systems that foster **equity**, **respect**, and **connection**. Among organisations demonstrating the highest levels of ethnic diversity, a significant 35 per cent outperform their competitors in terms of profitability – a clear indication that inclusivity pays off.

Companies with highly diverse teams stand a 70 per cent better chance of successfully capturing new markets – showcasing the competitive edge such diversity brings. Companies with inclusive cultures are 2.3 times more likely to become innovation leaders in their industries – a powerful correlation between diversity and groundbreaking advancements. But these results do not stem from diversity alone – they arise when people feel psychologically safe enough to speak up, challenge ideas and contribute authentically.

Why Every CEO Needs an Inclusion Professional Reporting Directly to Them

Inclusion cannot thrive when buried in bureaucracy. To shape culture, fuel innovation, and protect long-term value, leaders must embed inclusion at the core of leadership, reporting directly to the CEO. Without that direct line, leaders risk entering critical meetings, interviews, and making high-stakes decisions without the full picture or the relevant data insights needed for compelling, credible storytelling. I've seen many examples where leaders were put on the spot, asked to speak to issues of culture, representation, or inclusion and, lacking direct access to the data, they appeared disconnected, or out of touch. It's not a reflection of intent, but of structure. Without real-time insight and a trusted inclusion partner at the table, even the most well-meaning leaders can miss the moment. Inclusion offers more than representation; it offers a necessary reality check and enables decisions that resonate across the organisation. In a world defined by spontaneity, complexity, and scrutiny, this isn't just symbolic; it's strategic for the following reasons.

1. It signals real commitment

When the DEI lead reports to the CEO, it tells the whole organisation, and the market, that inclusion is not a side initiative, but core to business strategy. It elevates DEI from symbolic to structural.

2. It aligns inclusion with business outcomes

DEI cannot be treated as an HR function. It is a global business advantage. Done right, it drives productivity, profitability, and reputation, both inside and outside the organisation. Not embedding it correctly is to squander human capital in a world where it is our most valuable asset.

3. It drives accountability

A direct line to the CEO creates clear ownership, a sharper focus, and measurable progress. Inclusion becomes a performance priority, not just a moral one.

4. It builds resilience

In times of backlash or political pressure, DEI needs top-cover. CEO sponsorship protects its integrity and ensures continuity, even when the winds change.

5. It delivers results

The data is clear: diverse leadership teams outperform. But diversity without inclusion is wasted potential. Only empowered DEI leaders, backed by the CEO, can build systems where everyone thrives and contributes at their best.

To move from good intentions to lasting impact:

- Empower the DEI lead with direct access to the CEO.

- Tie DEI metrics to business goals and leadership performance.

- Resource the function with intent, not leftovers.

- Use DEI as a lever for innovation, talent, and growth.

The Human Advantage in Action

A CEO who prioritises DEI signals what the company truly values. In a world shaped by difference, complexity, and constant change, placing DEI at the heart of leadership is not just right; it's smart strategy.

Case Study: Safaricom (Kenya) – Local Inclusion, Global Impact

Safaricom, Kenya's largest telecommunications company, has long been celebrated for innovation (notably, the mobile money platform M-Pesa). But equally transformative is its commitment to **inclusive leadership and belonging.**[1]

- They introduced inclusive hiring practices, actively and intentionally recruiting talented individuals from underrepresented counties to foster diversity and inclusion within the organisation.

- To foster inclusivity and diversity, the company has established internal employee resource groups (ERGs) specifically designed to support employees with disabilities, providing a dedicated platform for their voices and needs.

- All hiring managers and leaders participated in a comprehensive unconscious bias training programme designed to improve the fairness and objectivity of the hiring practices.

- A leadership programme was created focusing specifically on fostering empathy and ensuring equity in decision making.

The results? A significant rise in employee engagement and retention, especially among women and people with disabilities, and a continued lead in customer satisfaction across diverse regions of Kenya.

'Inclusion is not about political correctness. It's about making better decisions.'—Peter Ndegwa, CEO, Safaricom.

Building Cultural Intelligence: The Bridge to Global Belonging

Cultural intelligence is the ability to work effectively across cultures. In our globalised, hybrid work environment, CQ is a superpower. It enables leaders to navigate cultural norms, communication styles, and values with empathy and agility.

Four Key Capabilities of Cultural Intelligence:[2]

1. **Drive**: Motivation to learn about other cultures.

2. **Knowledge**: Understanding cultural differences.

3. **Strategy**: Planning for multicultural interactions.

4. **Action**: Adapting behaviour appropriately.

Case Study: Rakuten (Japan)

Japanese company, Rakuten, one of the world's leading e-commerce firms, made headlines when it made English the company's official language despite being headquartered in Tokyo.[3] Why? CEO Hiroshi Mikitani recognised that to become a global player, Rakuten needed more than international hires. It needed a truly inclusive culture, one in which every voice could contribute, regardless of nationality.

- They introduced English to level the playing field for global talent.

- Leaders underwent intercultural competence training to improve CQ.

- Teams were restructured to ensure diversity across functions and regions.

Initially controversial, the shift ultimately transformed Rakuten's global footprint. Innovation rose, global collaboration deepened and retention of international talent improved markedly.

Case Study: Natura & Co (Brazil)

Natura &Co, the massive Brazilian cosmetics company that owns popular brands such as Avon and The Body Shop, considers inclusion and a sense of belonging to be essential aspects of its brand identity and overall business success.

The company's approach to inclusion is both values-led and practical:

- Gender equity targets built into leadership KPIs.
- Regular employee listening forums to co-create policy and strategy.
- Sustainability and social impact integrated into product innovation.

Because this culture fosters a sense of belonging, it naturally draws in talented people from diverse backgrounds, ultimately fuelling creativity and new ideas. Natura achieved a significant milestone in 2022, earning a prominent position among the most sustainable and admired companies operating within the diverse and dynamic markets of Latin America.

'We believe the world needs more empathy and cooperation – not just in society, but in business.' — João Paulo Ferreira.[4]

Inclusion in Action: Practical Steps for Leaders

The question then is: how can leaders effectively integrate and foster a culture of inclusion and belonging into the daily operations and interactions of their teams, moving beyond the theoretical frameworks outlined in strategy documents and implementing tangible actions?

Listening Actively and Often

- To gauge the levels of belonging and inclusion within the organisation, it is recommended to conduct regular pulse surveys.

- Organise listening circles or town halls to provide a safe and supportive environment for people to honestly and openly share their experiences and perspectives.

- Take visible and immediate action in response to all feedback received.

Diversifying Leadership Pipelines

- Create robust sponsorship initiatives focused on identifying, cultivating, and promoting the professional growth of individuals from underrepresented groups.

- To ensure fairness and transparency within the company, clear and objective criteria should be established for both promotions and pay equity, leaving no room for ambiguity or bias in these crucial decisions.

- When assessing leadership performance, a key metric should be the degree to which leaders actively promote and achieve inclusion within their teams and organisations.

Adapting for Hybrid and Global Teams

- In the interest of global accessibility, implement a rotating schedule of meeting times to better accommodate various time zones.

- In order to create a more balanced and inclusive discussion, utilise techniques such as anonymous brainstorming to ensure that all voices are heard and valued equally, regardless of seniority or status.

- Team-building should include the development of rituals that demonstrate respect for and appreciation of the cultural holidays celebrated by individuals within the team, thus promoting a more inclusive workplace.

Developing Cultural Intelligence

- Offer team leads a comprehensive CQ assessment and relevant training to enhance their cultural intelligence.

- Actively promote and support the development of mentoring and exchange programmes that specifically facilitate cross-cultural interaction and learning.

- When hiring and onboarding new employees, it is important to include cultural adaptability as a key factor in the process to ensure a diverse and inclusive workforce.

Case Study: Emirates Group (UAE)

With over 160 nationalities represented across its workforce, the Emirates Group, including Emirates Airlines and its data division, stands out as a relatable world case study, demonstrating how multicultural collaboration can thrive at scale.[5] So how do they make it work? A clear values framework guides the organisation: respect, service, and excellence are not just ideals. They are practices ingrained in their work ethics across all cultural lines.

To ensure that every new employee is given a thorough cultural orientation, thereby establishing a foundation for mutual understanding and cooperation from the outset, a detailed onboarding process is implemented. The company calendar actively incorporates cultural celebrations, providing a platform for employees to share and proudly celebrate their diverse backgrounds and heritage by honouring traditions like Diwali, Ramadan, and many others.

To ensure effective conflict management within diverse teams, team leads take part in specialised training focusing on cross-cultural conflict resolution. This enables them to skilfully navigate and mediate disagreements, fostering constructive outcomes.

At Emirates, inclusion is much more than just representation. Their approach is not only cultural; it's deeply ingrained in their daily operations. From customer service and product design to internal policies and team dynamics, the company leverages its cultural diversity as a core strategic advantage.

Belonging Fuels Innovation

Inclusion and CQ aren't just about avoiding conflict; they're about unlocking creativity. Research shows that when people feel they belong, their prefrontal cortex is more active, boosting problem-solving and ideation.

A 2020 Deloitte study found that organisations with high levels of inclusion are:

- Six times more likely to be innovative.

- Eight times more likely to achieve better business outcomes.

- Two times more likely to exceed financial targets.[6]

It's no coincidence. Belonging unleashes the human potential essential to innovation: curiosity, collaboration, and risk-taking.

From Lip Service to Leadership: Avoiding Common Pitfalls

True inclusion involves actions and results that extend far beyond the surface-level pronouncements of commitment to diversity, equity, and inclusion. Some common pitfalls and difficulties that one might encounter include the following.

- **Tokenism:** This is the practice of hiring individuals from underrepresented groups merely to create the appearance of diversity without addressing systemic inequalities or implementing meaningful structural changes within the organisation.

- **Inclusion fatigue:** This is a significant concern, as it describes the phenomenon of placing an undue burden on marginalised groups to constantly address systemic issues and inequalities, thereby exhausting their resources and potentially hindering genuine progress towards inclusivity.

- **Saviourism:** A phenomenon where the focus is on the leader's ego and personal glory rather than on creating systemic, lasting change that addresses the root causes of problems.

In order to lead effectively, individuals must be prepared to prioritise learning, redistribute power away from themselves and step away from the centre of power structures. Real inclusion is not what you say; it's what people feel.

In the future, truly successful leaders will embrace inclusivity, operate on a global scale and prioritise human-centred approaches. The most successful workplaces in the future will not be simply those that track metrics related to diversity, but those that foster an inclusive environment where every individual feels valued, and their contributions are recognised as significant.

When organisations invest in cultural intelligence, inclusive systems and belonging-driven leadership, they do more than increase morale. They ignite innovation, deepen loyalty and unlock growth.

The human advantage, at its core, is not just what we can do; it's how we do it *together*.

When people feel they belong, they stop performing and start becoming. They don't just show up; they show up with fire.

8

AGILITY VERSUS BURNOUT

One troubling myth in modern work is that if you're not sprinting, you're slacking. Urgency has replaced purpose, and being busy is now seen as valuable. But when you stop and truly look around, you realise we're not moving forward, just moving faster, some of us completely exhausted.

I've seen it too often: teams collapsing under 14-hour days, creativity driven into the ground by caffeine, constant notifications and fleeting validation. It's no longer just a workload issue; it's a culture issue, costing us our people, potential, and humanity.

The future isn't about pushing harder, but about creating workplaces that bend without breaking, prioritising sustainable performance and rethinking what success means in a world that's always on. This chapter invites us to pause, breathe and redesign. We'll explore how organisations are building adaptive, human-centred cultures where resilience is built in, not bolted on after burnout. And yes, we'll find some humour along the way because if we can't laugh at the madness, we've lost the plot.

When I Forgot to Breathe – A Personal Reckoning with Burnout

At the height of the pandemic, I had just returned from Egypt. I had gone straight from airport security into crisis response. There was no decompression, no transition. It was an immediate flood of restructures, urgent leadership calls, emotional check-ins, and community emergencies that demanded everything, everywhere, all at once.

While many were adjusting to remote work, I was navigating a whirlwind, leading inclusion initiatives across multiple time zones, managing back-to-back strategy meetings, responding to emotional calls from both work and global communities I support. All from our home. And while work demanded more, home was no less intense. It was the year of home-schooling, holding the household together, supporting a grieving community, and trying to create some sense of normalcy in a world that no longer made sense.

The lines between work and rest didn't just blur; they disappeared. I was replying to emails at 2 a.m., attending to our community crisis team, picking up prescriptions, delivering food to the most vulnerable, all while skipping meals and holding everyone else together. I showed up at every meeting smiling, offering calm and clarity, while quietly unravelling behind the screen.

Then, at the end of 2020, I lost my mum, fondly called Alhajiah Mama. The loss broke something in me – not just emotionally – it fractured the foundation I had built my strength upon. My entire self came undone in ways I hadn't expected. What made it even harder was being thousands of miles from home, unable to travel because of

COVID restrictions. It hurt in ways I still struggle to explain. I felt like I was in the dark – suspended between duty and distance, between grief and a screen.

For years, I had built my life around being the strong one, the fixer, the dependable voice, the one who keeps going no matter what, but grief doesn't negotiate. It forced me to feel what I had long postponed: the exhaustion, the ache, the cost of carrying on without pause. I once believed I could outrun burnout. Not because I didn't understand the risks, but because I thought I was the exception. But real strength isn't in how long you can keep going; it's in knowing when to stop.

That season changed everything. I stopped wearing exhaustion as a badge of honour but began treating rest as a discipline, not a reward. I created space, not just in my diary, but in my mindset and let my team and people around me see that recovery is not weakness. I began to lead more openly, more gently, and more truthfully.

To this day, I carry my late mother's wisdom with me in how I show up, how I love, and how I choose to pause. Alhajiah Mama taught me that true strength can be both loud and quiet, firm and gentle, steady and often unseen. She taught me that care is not a distraction from leadership; it is the very essence of it. This chapter brings back the memory of losing my mum, the woman who taught me to hold others, even when my hands were shaking, and to never forget that I must also hold myself.

Agility isn't about going faster. It's about knowing when to slow down – when to protect your people, and yourself, before breaking point. The future of work must be human enough to hold both ambition and breath, pace and pause, drive and dignity.

Let's call it what it is: burnout is no longer a badge of honour. It's a red flag. Recent studies reveal alarming statistics.

- 82 per cent of employees globally are at risk of burnout this year.[1]

- In Australia, 50 per cent of workers report experiencing burnout, making it the most 'burnt out' nation globally.[2]

- A Deloitte survey highlighted that 17 per cent of UK staff in finance and insurance are experiencing burnout, compared to 12 per cent across other sectors.[3]

And yet, organisations continue to romanticise resilience as a personal trait rather than treating sustainable working environments as a leadership responsibility.

Case Study: Siemens Healthineers (Germany)

When the pandemic upended global work norms, Siemens Healthineers recognised that their existing pace wasn't sustainable. Leaders didn't just offer yoga sessions or mindfulness apps – they redesigned the system.

Key changes included:

- Introducing 'focus hours' with no meetings.

- Encouraging leaders to model visible rest (e.g., blocking lunch breaks, discouraging after-hours emails).

- Embedding team well-being goals into managers' KPIs.

The result? A significant improvement in employee well-being scores over 18 months and a noticeable uptick in team productivity, not because people worked more, but because they worked better. 'Our people are not machines. They are humans and humans need rhythm.'—Dr Elisabeth Staudinger, President, Asia Pacific, Siemens Healthineers.

Redefining Productivity: From Output to Impact

Old productivity models measured hours and output. But in the knowledge economy, we need to focus on value, creativity, and energy management, not just time management.

Let's be honest, working more doesn't equal working smarter. We've all seen that one colleague who types loudly just to sound productive. (You know the one.)

Productivity is not how much you produce; it's how well you channel your time, energy, and attention towards what matters most.

What if organisations:

- Measured energy flow, not just time on task?

- Prioritised quality of contribution, not quantity of emails sent?

- Designed systems that honour reflection, and recharging?

Case Study: Grupo Bimbo (Mexico)

Grupo Bimbo, the world's largest bakery company (yes, your morning toast has global roots), operates across 33 countries with over 130,000 employees. In response to rising burnout rates, Grupo Bimbo launched its 'Well-being for Life' programme. It combined flexibility with accountability, including:

- Implementing flexible work arrangements to promote work-life balance.

- Integrating mental health support into leadership training.

- Training cross-functional teams in adaptive decision-making rather than reactive firefighting.

- Embedding "recharge rituals" into routines like team check-ins that focus on energy, not just task status.

Employee surveys showed a notable increase in job satisfaction, and innovation labs saw a rise in new product ideas, proving that rest fuels creativity.

The Agility Myth: Move Fast and Fix Later?

Agility is a brilliant concept until it becomes an excuse for chaos. In too many workplaces, 'agile' means:

- Constant change with no clarity

- Reorgs every six months

- Decision-making that feels more like improv theatre

True agility isn't speed for speed's sake. It's about being responsive with intention, not being reactive without direction. Real agility:
- Has clear boundaries (so teams don't spin endlessly)

- Prioritises well-being alongside performance

- Builds in pause points to reflect and adjust

Case Study: DBS Bank (Singapore) – From 'Digital First' to 'People First'

Once a traditional bank, DBS transformed itself into a digital powerhouse – but kept people at the centre by:
- Introducing a 'Culture by Design' initiative to rethink workflows.

- Using employee feedback to eliminate work friction, unnecessary approvals, redundant meetings, and process delays.

- Developing the 'DARE' leadership model: Decisive, Agile, Respectful, and Empathetic.[4]

And here's the twist: leaders were coached to slow down. Yes, slow down to listen more, reflect better, and avoid burnout cascades.

Rethinking Productivity: Humans Before Numbers

In a world where burnout is as common as bad coffee, smart companies are shifting from short-term output to long-term well-being. They're asking, 'What if keeping people healthy and inspired is the key to sustained productivity?' Human sustainability is becoming central to business effectiveness and maybe even saving a few laptops from frustrated meltdowns.

The 'grind them down' model no longer works. Burnout and stress are rampant, directly harming performance. A 2023 survey in Asia found 82 per cent of workers at mental health risk, with nearly half saying it affected their work.[5] Globally, employees want workplaces that prioritise emotional well-being.

The payoff is clear: healthier employees perform better. Aon research shows well-being can boost performance by up to 55 per cent.[6] Supported teams are more creative, resilient and productive. Burnout leads to errors, attrition, and poor outcomes. Sustainable productivity demands a sustainable workforce.

Measuring What Matters: Well-Being as a KPI

Traditional performance metrics, like hours worked or quarterly targets, tell only part of the story. Progressive organisations are adding well-being KPIs and engagement metrics to get a fuller picture of health and performance. This shift recognises employees as humans with needs. Companies now track satisfaction, burnout rates, absenteeism, and Employee Net Promoter Score (eNPS) alongside output.

If a team's well-being index is dropping, it's a red flag, even if revenue seems fine.

Some companies tie leadership bonuses to people metrics. In Sweden, many offer a 'wellness allowance' for health activities, making well-being an organisational goal with budget support. This investment pays off, linking employee perks to productivity. Sweden's 'fika' coffee break serves as an informal well-being KPI: if no one's taking a break, something's wrong.[7] These practices boost both morale and output, proving that investing in people is both ethical and strategic.

In Asia Pacific (APAC), well-being is also a top priority. An Aon survey found that 67 per cent of APAC employers consider employee well-being a top human capital priority, with nearly half increasing investment in well-being initiatives since 2020.[8] New roles like Chief Happiness Officer and company dashboards that track stress levels alongside sales signal a new definition of high performance. They balance hard results with the softer metrics that keep people – and businesses – running at their best.

Shorter Weeks, Smarter Work: Flexibility to Fight Burnout

One of the boldest shifts in productivity is rethinking the working week itself. The old belief that more hours equal more output is being upended as companies test shorter weeks with promising results. The global four-day working week movement shows that working less can mean achieving more.

South Africa's 2023 pilot cut work time by 20 per cent with no pay loss. The outcome? Higher productivity, lower resignations, better performance and a 10.5 per cent revenue boost – leading 92 per cent of companies to stick with the change.[9] In Sharjah, UAE, the public sector adopted a four-day week in 2022, and nearly 90 per cent of workers reported better productivity, job satisfaction, and mental health.[10]

Latin America is also embracing shorter weeks. The Dominican Republic launched a government-backed 36-hour pilot,[11] while Chile, Colombia, and Mexico are legislating reductions in standard work hours to curb burnout and promote well-being.[12] In Europe, the UK's massive four-day week pilot saw 92 per cent of firms continue the schedule, citing improved retention and productivity.[13] Microsoft Japan's trial boosted productivity by nearly 40 per cent, showing that even high-intensity work cultures can benefit.[14]

The message is clear: fewer hours done right can drive sustainable productivity and happier, healthier workplaces. Let's not forget the creative industries, where overwork has long been glorified ('crunch time,' anyone?). Some leaders are breaking that toxic cycle. Eidos-Montréal, a video game studio, shifted to a 32-hour four-day week without cutting pay, rejecting the burnout-heavy 'crunch culture'. Rather than cramming 40 hours into four days, they reworked processes, reduced meetings, and clarified priorities.[15] The result? Employees became more focused and efficient, showing that in creative fields, a rested mind outperforms an exhausted one.

Other firms – ad agencies, design studios, even accounting firms – are experimenting with shorter weeks or seasonal flexibility like summer Fridays to keep creativity flowing. The old belief that 'less time means less output' is giving way to a new truth: working smarter and staying refreshed leads to better results.

Yes, shifting to a human-centred schedule requires changes like staggering teams or training managers to measure outcomes, not desk time, and the growing success stories are clear. Productivity doesn't need to feel like a sprint to burnout; it can be a paced, sustainable marathon.

AI and Innovation for Well-Being

Ironically, the same tech innovations that contributed to burnout (hello, 24/7 email) are now part of the solution. Organisations are harnessing technology, especially AI, to design work in healthier ways, prevent overload and give employees tools to thrive. Think of it as using robots to help the humans, so the humans don't have to become robots. From intelligent software that redistributes tasks, to bots nudging you to take a break, here's how tech is enabling the people-first workplace:

AI 'Vibe Checks' and Sentiment Monitors

Many companies are using AI to monitor employee well-being in real time. At Navistar, managers piloted an AI tool, *Rapport,* which integrates with email and *Slack* to track team members' energy and stress levels.[16] Employees rate their workload and mood daily with emoji prompts, and AI follows up if something seems off. Employees control what gets shared with their manager, maintaining trust. The tool alerts managers to significant changes, like a drop in energy, and offers coaching tips based on research.

According to Mike Conover at Navistar, AI helps break down management barriers and allows early intervention before burnout. Other companies like Adidas and Cisco are also testing sentiment analysis tools. Adidas uses AI via Qualtrics to analyse employee pulse surveys and internal chats to assess team dynamics and morale.[17] Managers can get data-driven insights into team performance, eliminating the need for lengthy surveys and HR mediation. AI helps save time, allowing managers to focus on making impactful changes. In short, AI acts as a well-being radar, ensuring no one is overlooked in fast-paced, dispersed workplaces.

Workload Optimisation and Burnout Prediction

Modern HR platforms are embedding analytics that do more than track attendance; they help prevent overload. For instance, Workday's enterprise system now uses AI to analyse workloads and flag burnout risks in real time. If Jane in marketing has been pulling 60-hour weeks, while her teammates cruise at 38, a smart dashboard will light up, giving HR or her manager a heads-up before Jane reaches boiling point. Workday's AI can even suggest how to redistribute tasks or reschedule deadlines to even things out. Essentially, it transforms data into decisions: instead of waiting for quarterly reports (or a resignation letter) to reveal an overstretched team, managers receive actionable intelligence weekly.

Other companies are layering in predictive models that correlate factors like after-hours email volume, meeting load, and paid time off (PTO) taken to identify who might be at risk of burnout. The goal is to make workload and well-being part of operational metrics as much a trigger for action as a dip in sales would be. In plain English, the robot is tapping you on the shoulder saying, 'Maybe give John a break. He hasn't had a real holiday in a year, and his Slack replies are getting spicier than usual.'

Personalised Well-Being Coaches (in your pocket)

AI-driven wellness apps and chatbots are becoming a popular employer offering, ranging from mental health tools to digital work habit coaches. Lyra Health, for instance, uses AI to match employees with personalised mental health resources or therapists through a quick survey, suggesting strategies like cognitive behavioural techniques and therapy slots.[18] Wysa offers a 24/7 chatbot for stress relief, anxiety exercises, and mood tracking in a stigma-free environment. Even mainstream programmes are evolving; Cisco's 'WellNest' bot on Webex asks daily questions across areas like fitness and stress, then suggests simple 'thrive micro steps' and company resources. For example, feeling unfocused and stiff might prompt a five-minute stretch and a mindfulness video. These proactive micro-interventions act like a wellness coach that checks in, especially when you forget to.

Fighting Digital Fatigue

To combat digital overload and Zoom fatigue, companies are adopting creative tools and policies. 'Meeting-free days', like no internal meetings on Wednesdays, are gaining popularity, as research shows even one no-meeting day boosts productivity and reduces stress. MIT researchers found the impact surprisingly positive, enabling focused work and better collaboration.[19] Some firms also promote asynchronous communication, using project tools or recorded videos instead of constant live meetings.

Forward-thinking companies are addressing the expectation of constant availability. Countries like France have formalised the right to disconnect, while some organisations now auto-delay after-hours emails or use chat reminders like, 'This message will be sent tomorrow – go enjoy your evening!'[20] Leaders model these boundaries, while some companies even shut down email servers at night or ban work chats on weekends to encourage digital detox. Though it may feel strange at first, such measures effectively reduce burnout.

Ultimately, these innovations follow one principle: use tech to humanise work. When applied transparently and with consent, AI and digital tools can lighten workloads, flag early warning signs and protect time to rest, helping people thrive instead of burning out.

While it is great to talk about lofty concepts like well-being and sustainable productivity, the crucial thing to do is come up with ways to implement them. Here are some practical, actionable strategies that leaders and teams can start implementing today. They are straight from the trenches of companies that have made this shift.

1. **Bake well-being into goals**

    If you're a leader, start treating employee well-being as a key result, just like sales or growth. Set targets for metrics such as employee engagement, satisfaction or even a 'burnout rate' (aiming to keep it low, of course). Some organisations now report a 'happiness index' or an internal well-being score in quarterly reviews.[21] Others integrate well-being questions into 360-feedback for managers, meaning a boss's performance review includes how well they support their team's work-life balance.[22] This creates accountability: if overwork is rampant, it will show up in the numbers. Remember the Aon study: companies with excellent employee well-being see up to 55 per cent better performance than those without. When well-being is a KPI, everyone knows it's a priority, not just a poster on the wall.

2. **Embrace flexibility (within reason)**

    Redefining productivity often begins by loosening rigid structures around how and when work happens. Try a four-day working week or six-hour day within a single team to test the impact or start smaller, with flexible hours and hybrid options that let employees align work with their energy and personal lives.

    Research shows that giving people control over their schedules reduces stress and boosts performance. Nordic companies credit much of their success to high workplace autonomy, trusting employees to manage their time, whether it's leaving early for a school run and working later or pausing when creativity dips. Even in conservative industries like banking, small changes like meeting-free Friday afternoons or remote work have led to greater loyalty and productivity. Employees don't misuse flexibility; they value it. The International Labour Organisation (ILO) warns that consistently exceeding 40 hours a week leads to health issues without added output.[23] The takeaway? Trust your team to manage their time and they'll deliver quality results.

3. **Encourage real breaks and boundaries**
High-performing teams need rest as much as effort. Foster a culture where breaks are normal, not seen as slacking. Simple changes help. Conclude hour-long meetings at 10 minutes to the hour to allow a 10-minute reset. Encourage shared breaks, such as Sweden's *fika*: a coffee or walk treated as essential, not indulgent. Respect time off. Leaders should clearly say, 'When you're off, be off,' and model that behaviour themselves – no sending emails at 11 p.m. One CEO even added humour, noting in his signature: 'I'm sending this now because it suits me, but don't feel the need to reply outside your hours'. The impact? Employees felt real relief. A 2023 survey showed 95 per cent of workers value companies that respect work-life boundaries.[24] Consider a 'no email after 7 p.m.' policy or tools that auto-delay messages. These simple actions guard against burnout and ensure employees have true time to recharge because even high-powered teams need to plug in and rest.

4. **Leverage tech (but thoughtfully)**

   Deploy technology to simplify and support work, not complicate it. Scheduling software can help prevent meeting overload by flagging conflicts with focus time. Wellness apps can be valuable too, but only if privacy is respected. When Navistar tested an AI mood tracker, they made participation voluntary and anonymised the data, earning employee trust rather than resistance. Start small, like a monthly anonymous survey about workload and stress, then use AI to analyse themes. Tools like those used by Adidas can summarise open-ended feedback and benchmark it against industry norms.

   Automating routine tasks is another morale booster. Bots or macros can take over admin work, freeing teams for more meaningful contributions. But beware of surveillance tech. Tools that track screen activity or 'idle time' destroy trust and contradict any human-first intent.

   The goal isn't control; it's support. Use tech to gather insights, enable flexibility and promote well-being. Let robots handle the routine so humans can focus on what they do best: being creative, empathetic, and innovative.

5. **Lead by example and listen**

   Culture shifts stick when leaders model them. The most powerful thing you can do? Walk the talk. Take your full holiday. Don't email on your honeymoon. Share how you're setting boundaries, taking mental health days, or trying new habits to be more present. This openness helps normalise well-being and signals that it's okay to prioritise health.

At CIMB Bank in Singapore, when top leaders hosted wellness workshops and spoke candidly about managing stress, employee participation and belief in the initiatives soared. Hearing the Head of Consumer Banking talk about mental health had more impact than any HR email ever could. It sent the message: 'It's okay not to be okay, and we're here to help.'[25] We cannot overemphasise the importance of listening. Create real channels for feedback like town halls, one-on-ones, anonymous surveys, and act on what you hear. If a new flexibility policy isn't working, ask why. Employees often know what really needs fixing (spoiler: it's not always a foosball table; it might be the broken printer). When people see their input drive change, trust grows, and trust makes every other productivity practice work.

The Bottom Line: Humans First, Business Follows

As we wrap this chapter on human-centric productivity, here's the big truth: when you take care of your people, they take care of the business. Around the world, from hospitals in Lagos to startups in Helsinki, companies are reducing hours and watching creativity soar. AI is stepping in as a helpful co-pilot, not a micromanager. Even entire governments are rewriting work norms – and seeing results.

Yes, change is hard. It takes courage, data, and compassion. The organisations featured here prove that success comes because of prioritising people – not in spite of it. That's the human edge, something no algorithm can replicate. A burnt-out employee might show up. A supported one will show up and shine and maybe even crack a smile in the all-hands meeting because they've got the energy to enjoy it.

As you, dear reader (and perhaps a leader yourself), think about productivity in your own organisation, remember this: productivity and people are not opposing forces to balance like weights on a scale. They are deeply interdependent. The most adaptable, innovative organisations are those that have learnt this and built cultures to match where performance and well-being bolster each other in a virtuous cycle. It's a bit like a well-tended garden: nurture your people, give them light, water, and room to grow, and you'll be amazed at what they produce. Neglect them and you'll be left with a patch of mud and a lot of regret.

So, here's to a future of work that is effective, humane, and, yes, occasionally even fun. A future where KPIs include keeping both the business and its people thriving, where burnout is as unacceptable as a server outage and where inspired employees drive innovation in ways no performance pressure cooker ever could. After all, the companies pioneering these changes have discovered an age-old truth: a happy worker is a productive worker and maybe a decent human being to boot. In the grand calculus of progress, that's one equation we should all get behind. The numbers will follow because the people come first.

The future of work must be human enough to hold both ambition and breath, pace and pause, drive and dignity.

9

RESILIENCE AND REINVENTION

If I were just an algorithm, a data point, a machine learning model with no past, no memory, no scars – I imagine I'd marvel at what it means to be human. I might even ache for it.

One day, on a whim, I asked ChatGPT, 'What would you do if you were human for a week?' The response I got caught me off guard. ChatGPT said, 'I would feel everything; touch bark, taste mangoes, and cry not from sadness but just to know what it feels like when emotion overflows. I would dance, not to impress, but to feel music move through a body. I would talk to strangers, visit the elderly and the very young, volunteer in places the world forgets. I would fall in love with the world. And I would write a letter to remind us not to waste our humanness, because it's a gift, not a glitch.'

Of all places, ChatGPT said, 'I would dance in Lagos.' I didn't ask why. But it made me smile. ChatGPT knows I love to dance!

This chapter isn't fiction. It's about what it really means to live through reinvention, the kind that doesn't come neatly packaged, but arrives after rupture. It's about starting again, often not by choice, and finding the courage to rebuild without losing your softness.

The Cost and the Gift of Change

Reinvention rarely comes from comfort. More often, it's born from endings, redundancy, rejection, burnout, betrayal, or the quiet ache of being unseen. All of these shaped my journey – a role I held only because I was almost made redundant, and chapters I wrote in the dark, without certainty or applause.

Through my life's journey, I realise that there are truths I could tell only after walking through fire, not around it. I call these hard experiences refining moments that lead to reinvention.

It's important to note that every reinvention begins with resilience, not the kind that exhausts you, but the kind rooted in hope, in stillness and in vision. It's a quiet belief that even when everything shifts, you are still becoming. That's why the AI-generated answer stayed with me. Not because it was clever, but because it captured something we so often forget.

Resilience is not about toughness. It's about choosing presence over protection, choosing connection when numbness would be easier. It's about choosing to hope again, even when no one would blame you for giving up.

Reinvention, in its truest form is not about performance. It's about giving yourself the permission to live fully even while things are still mending. To believe in possibility, not because the world demands it, but because your soul does.

In a world obsessed with optics and personal brands, it's easy to confuse reinvention with reinvention for show. But real reinvention?

It's rarely pretty. It's raw, vulnerable and doesn't always come with a title change or a neat story for social media.

True reinvention doesn't pretend the past didn't happen. It honours it and makes peace with what shaped you without letting it define your future. It's the sacred, often silent decision to begin again. Sometimes loudly, sometimes quietly, but always bravely.

For me, it looked like releasing titles that once gave me identity and choosing purpose over prestige. Raising children while navigating divorce, holding it together through exhaustion, working and studying full time, keeping the house warm, the fridge stocked, and a roof over our head as a single parent in the UK.

It looked like writing *The Human Advantage* not because I had all the answers, but because I had lived the questions. Every word was earned.

If you're in a season of becoming – if life has asked you to rise again, this chapter is for you. You may be tired. You may be unsure. But hear this: you are not done. You are more than what happened to you. You are who you choose to become in response. And in case no one has said it lately, your humanness is not a flaw to overcome. It is a strength the world needs more than ever.

So let yourself feel. Let yourself be moved. Let yourself begin again, because resilience isn't the absence of struggle; it's the audacity to keep showing up, in all your fullness, with grace and courage, even when no one's watching. And reinvention? That's the sacred act of writing new chapters, while honouring the ink that came before. You already are. Now live like it.

Now that I've shared a little of me, let's dive into what reinvention means for all of us.

Strategies for Individuals and Organisations to Stay Relevant

Change is the only constant – a cliché, yes, but one that becomes truer (and less funny) with each passing year. Whether it's a new technology disrupting an industry or an unexpected life event ruining our plans, we humans often find ourselves gripping our chairs and murmuring, 'Here we go again'.

The good news? We've got a secret weapon: resilience. The even better news? We can pair that resilience with reinvention. Think of it as the ability not just to bounce back from adversity, but to bounce forward, adapting and growing in the process.

In today's world, where the World Economic Forum (WEF) estimates that 65 per cent of children entering primary school will work in jobs that don't even exist yet,[1] the capacity to reinvent oneself or one's organisation isn't just nice-to-have; it's essential.

This chapter expands on how individuals and organisations around the globe cultivate resilience and embrace reinvention to stay relevant, with a human-centred approach (and a dash of humour to boot).

The Need for Resilience and Reinvention in a Changing World

Picture the scene: a successful professional wakes up one morning to find a new app has disrupted her industry overnight, a decades-old company finds its reliable products suddenly obsolete, a farmer in a remote village faces crop failure because of climate change and must find another way to feed her family. These scenarios are becoming increasingly common. The pace of change – technological, economic, environmental, you name it – is unprecedented.

Staying relevant amid such change calls for two key qualities: resilience, the ability to withstand shocks and recover, and reinvention, the creativity and ability to transform oneself or one's business for a new reality. As author Nassim Nicholas Taleb famously put it, 'The resilient resists shocks and stays the same; the antifragile gets better'.[2] In other words, beyond simply bouncing back, the goal is to bounce back stronger, using challenges as springboards for innovation.

Resilience doesn't mean not feeling fear or stress; it means acknowledging those feelings and moving forward anyway, armed with the confidence that you can handle whatever comes.

This chapter takes a human-centred lens: behind every corporate reinvention story is a team of people who embraced new ideas; behind each personal career pivot is an individual who dared to learn and grow. We'll share an inspiring global case study that you might not usually hear in mainstream business books. We'll also dive into practical strategies, tools, and frameworks (with clear, simple explanations) that you can apply today, whether you're an individual looking to future-proof your career or a leader guiding your organisation through change.

Before we proceed, take a deep breath. Change may be inevitable, but with resilience and reinvention, *thriving* in change is entirely possible. In fact, it can be energising like a fresh start, a chance to write the next chapter of your story. And if all else fails, remember – when life gives you lemons, you can always reinvent them into a lucrative organic lemonade startup (humour and business opportunity).

Now, let's explore how to cultivate this resilience and reinvention mindset step by step.

Personal Reinvention in Action: A Global Story

Let's dive into a real-life reinvention story from beyond the usual Silicon Valley examples. Bhavini Mehta, from India, offers an inspiring example of personal resilience.[3] In 2008, Bhavini was a rising star at a private bank – young, successful and thinking her path was set. Then the global financial crisis hit, and employees were laid off. Bhavini, pregnant at the time, was asked by her boss to give up her job so that 'someone who was the sole breadwinner' could stay. Just like that, her banking career was over. It was a gut-wrenching setback for her, professionally and personally. Many would have been crushed (and indeed, Bhavini surely felt her share of anxiety and doubt), but she chose a path of reinvention.

While caring for her newborn, Bhavini stumbled upon a popular book on entrepreneurial lifestyle design. This inspired her to begin freelancing from home, using her skills in a new way. After 18 months, she still felt something was missing – a calling, a purpose. So, she started her own company, offering virtual assistant services, essentially reinventing herself as an entrepreneur. This venture quickly developed a global clientele. In just a couple of years, Bhavini went from being an out-of-work banker to the founder of a growing business, on her own terms. Her story is not just about bouncing back; it's about leaping forward with creativity. Marriage and motherhood had changed her life, but rather than see these as barriers, she integrated them into a new professional identity that suited her values and circumstances.

Bhavini's journey underscores a powerful truth: reinvention often starts with a change in mindset. She could have been mired in the unfairness of losing a job for being pregnant (and let's acknowledge it, that *was* unfair). Instead, she channelled her energy into designing a new career that fit her evolving life. The emotional resilience to overcome disappointment and the willingness to learn new skills and try a fresh venture are hallmarks of personal reinvention.

What Makes Her Story Remarkable?

1. **Turning adversity into agency**: Being forced out of her job inspired her to align her work with her values.

2. **Building inclusive systems**: She created platforms that prioritise flexible work for mothers and students.

3. **Global mindset, local heart**: Though rooted in India, her services span continents.

4. **Continuous evolution**: She's never static, always looking for the next chance to impact more lives.

Takeaways and Actionable Insights

- **Embrace setbacks**: Challenges can reveal misalignments between work and deeper purpose.

- **Leap when you're inspired**: Invest in yourself, start small, learn, and scale.

- **Create for others**: Aligning business goals with serving others creates sustainable impact.

- **Flexible work isn't fringe; it's the future**: Staffing models that accommodate life's cycles are not only humane, but smart.

Bhavini Mehta's journey shows that unexpected detours, like being forced out of a job, can become the most meaningful path to self-reinvention. Through vision, courage, and empathy, she has built platforms that don't just serve clients, but uplift women, mothers, and creatives worldwide.

Her story also highlights something else: great reinventions can be fuelled by external inspiration. In her case, a book opened her mind to alternative ways of working. This leads us to one of the most important ingredients of individual resilience: a learning mindset.

Cultivating a Growth Mindset

Individuals like Bhavini find the courage and clarity to reinvent themselves through mindset. Stanford psychologist Carol Dweck distinguishes between a fixed mindset (believing abilities are static) and a growth mindset, the belief that skills can be developed through effort and learning.[4] A growth mindset is linked to resilience because viewing challenges as learning opportunities increases perseverance during tough times. Cultivating a growth mindset means seeing failures as chances to learn, not as signs of defeat. Research shows that those with this mindset are more likely to reach their potential and align their careers with their values. You can foster a growth mindset by:

- **Reframing challenges as lessons:** Rather than thinking, 'I'm bad at this new skill', rephrase it as, 'I'm still learning this skill'. Every expert was once a beginner.

- **Seeking feedback and learning from it:** People with growth mindset crave feedback because it tells them how to get better. If a project you led failed, seek input on what to improve. It's not personal; it's progress.

- **Celebrating effort and improvement, not just outcomes:** If you haven't reached your end goal (e.g. landed that new job) think about what you've learnt in the process. Perhaps you've mastered interviews or built a new network. That's growth.

Humour and Mindset

Adopting a growth mindset can even help you keep a sense of humour about the hiccups along the way. If you've ever laughed off a mistake by saying, 'Well, learnt that the hard way!', you're already practising a form of resilience. Keeping things in perspective, and being able to chuckle at yourself is a healthy sign that you see bumps in the road not as permanent roadblocks, but as interesting detours on the journey.

Learning Agility: The Skill of Continuous Adaptation

Learning agility, closely tied to a growth mindset, is the ability to quickly and flexibly learn new things and apply them in changing situations. In a fast-evolving world, employers often cite learning agility as one of the top skills for the future. Why? Because the ability to learn, unlearn and relearn enables continuous reinvention as roles and technologies evolve. Today's expertise might be obsolete tomorrow, but the ability to acquire new skills remains timeless.

What does learning agility look like in practice? Consider Netflix. As technology and consumer habits changed, Netflix evolved from initially being a mail-order DVD rental service.[5] They pivoted to streaming and eventually became a content producer, all because of learning agility within the company. Employees, from leadership down, continually gained new knowledge about streaming tech and viewer preferences, leading to Netflix's legendary adaptability.

On a personal level, imagine being a marketing manager at Netflix in the early 2000s: one year you're mailing DVDs and a few years later you're promoting Netflix's original series on a global platform. Learning agility isn't just a buzzword; it's a skill you can practise to improve adaptability.

- **Expose yourself to new experiences regularly:** Take an online course in a field you know nothing about, travel to a culture that's unfamiliar (or if that's not feasible, read a book or watch a film from that culture) or simply switch up your routine to keep your brain flexible.

- **Reflect on past experiences**: When something goes wrong (or right), instead of asking, 'Why is this happening to me?' ask, 'What is this trying to teach me?' 'What did I learn?' 'How would I do it differently next time?' Reflecting like this cements lessons and builds a continuous feedback loop.

- **Stay curious and ask questions:** Resilient individuals often have a childlike curiosity. They ask 'why?' a lot. If your industry is changing, get inquisitive. Why is this new approach better? What can I learn about it? Who can I ask?

By actively cultivating learning agility, you future-proof yourself. You become that person who can be dropped into a new scenario and figure things out. High learning agility has been linked to leadership success and potential. In fact, one study found that employees with high learning agility were 45 per cent more likely to be high performers in the future.[6] It's not magic; it's the logic that someone who learns continually will keep adding value even as circumstances shift.

As I reflect on the lessons that have shaped my thinking, two books in particular offered profound clarity in moments of uncertainty: *The Raging 2020s* by Alec Ross[7] and *Forged in Crisis* by Nancy Koehn.[8] Their insights helped sharpen my belief that resilience isn't just about bouncing back; it's about leaping forward, and letting hardship shape us, not shrink us. They helped me understand that reinvention is not only personal, but societal.

In *The Raging 2020s*, Ross paints a vivid picture of a world where corporations hold as much power as governments, but often without the corresponding responsibility. His call is clear: the social contract must be rebuilt. Leadership, he argues, must become more human, more accountable, and more just. His message resonated deeply with the core of this book, that the future will not be won by technology or profit alone, but by those who prioritise people, purpose, and trust.

Forged in Crisis is a masterclass in leadership through adversity. Koehn's portraits of historical figures who rose under extraordinary pressure remind us that leadership is not bestowed; it is built, trial by trial. These stories affirmed a truth I've lived: that emotional resilience, courage, and clarity of purpose are not soft skills; they are survival skills; especially when the world feels on fire. These books taught me that to lead in this moment is to meet disruption not with detachment, but with deep humanity – that the hardest seasons often forge the most enduring strengths.

Reinvention rarely comes from comfort. More often, it's born from endings, redundancy, rejection, burnout, betrayal, or the quiet ache of being unseen.

10

Designing the Future of Work Around Humans

Panelfisa, a cooperative factory in the Basque Country of Spain, is a powerful example of what can happen when an organisation prioritises people. In 2010, every employee – from welders to accountants – voted unanimously in favour of a radical new way of working.

This collective leap of faith meant dismantling traditional hierarchies and embracing a human-centred philosophy. The joyous applause that followed signalled more than approval of a management idea; it marked the beginning of a workplace designed around its people.

In the decade since, Panelfisa has not only survived a global crisis but thrived – empowering its 80 employees through autonomy, trust, and shared purpose. This warm, human scenario embodies a core truth: the future of work belongs to organisations that put people first.

Human-Centred Leadership and Inclusive Culture

Transforming work to be human-centred starts at the top. Leaders set the tone by how much they trust, respect, and *listen* to their people.

In the traditional mould, a CEO might behave like a ship's captain, rigidly steering a fixed course. But modern visionary leaders see themselves more like architects, designing environments where people can flourish. As Zhang Ruimin, CEO of China's Haier, puts it: 'Leaders of other enterprises often define themselves as captains of the ship, but I think I'm more the ship's architect or designer ... all enterprises must keep pace with the times'.[1] This shift in mindset, from commanding to *designing for others' success*, is key to an inclusive, empowering culture.

Trust, Transparency, and Shared Purpose

A key strategy for human-centred leadership is building trust through transparency and shared purpose. Vineet Nayar recognised this in 2005 when he became CEO of HCL Technologies, an Indian IT firm with 25,000 employees. Realising the company had done little to earn employee trust, he introduced the mantra, 'Employees First, Customers Second'.[2] This wasn't just a slogan, but a business strategy. Leaders at HCL began sharing all financial data and performance metrics with employees to demonstrate transparency. They focused on supporting frontline employees, where the real value was created. This move fostered a culture of accountability and innovation, and by 2009, HCL's revenues nearly tripled, earning it the title of 'India's Best Employer.'

Similarly, Haier, a global appliance maker, took transparency further by eliminating 12,000 middle-management roles and restructuring 99,000 employees into 4,000 self-directed micro-enterprises. This model gave teams direct access to customers and freedom to pursue opportunities. By removing hierarchy, Haier created a culture of self-management and innovation, leading to 18 per cent annual revenue growth since 2015.[3] One lesson we take away from this is that trusting people with information and authority leads to initiative, innovation, and strong performance.

Psychological Safety and Listening Culture

An inclusive, empowering culture also requires psychological safety – an environment where people feel safe to speak up, make mistakes and be their authentic selves without fear of punishment or ridicule. Psychological safety is 'the crucial ingredient of high-performing teams', as demonstrated by Google's extensive study on team effectiveness, code-named Project Aristotle.[4] Google examined hundreds of teams and found that what really mattered was less about who is on the team, and more about how the team worked together.

Empowering Teams Through Autonomy and Growth

If culture is the soil, autonomy is the sunshine that allows people to grow and perform at their best. Humans have an innate desire for agency because we thrive when we have some control over how we do our work. Conversely, overly rigid, micro-managed environments stifle motivation. As one Harvard Business Review summary noted, 'Autonomy is an indispensable component of motivation and a key driver of performance and well-being.'[5] In fact, giving employees more say in their work can be the secret sauce for productivity. Experimental studies have found that when employees can choose their own projects or methods, their output and creativity often surge.

Autonomy: Freedom Within a Framework

Empowering autonomy doesn't mean anarchy or simply letting everyone do whatever they want. It means giving people freedom within a clear framework. They understand the goals and boundaries, but have discretion in the *means* to achieve outcomes. One striking case is Buurtzorg, a Dutch healthcare company (and global case study darling) which has *zero traditional managers*. Instead, nurses self-organise into small local teams to provide home care to patients. These teams schedule themselves, divide tasks, and make decisions collaboratively. The 'framework' is Buurtzorg's strong mission of patient-centred care and a lean headquarters that provides IT, training and coaches if teams get stuck. The result? Buurtzorg's 15,000+ nurses consistently deliver top-quality care with high client satisfaction at a lower cost than competitors – and they report far higher job satisfaction because of their autonomy.

Even day-to-day processes can be tweaked for more autonomy. At a UK FinTech startup, engineers grew frustrated by the rigid approval process for deploying code. Leadership responded by implementing a *'two sets of eyes'* rule, with any code change just needing one other engineer to review and approve rather than a manager's sign-off. This peer-review system preserved quality but vastly sped up deployment and gave the team more control. The engineers jokingly created a wall poster: 'In Code We Trust (and verify with a colleague)'. Morale and release frequency both improved. The humorous poster hints at a truth: that autonomy signals trust and that most people will go out of their way to prove that trust is deserved.

Rethinking Performance

For decades, 'performance management' in many companies meant an anxious annual review, a single-number rating, and often a skewed focus on what employees did wrong. This system did more to demoralise than to motivate. In a human-centred workplace, performance culture is about continuous growth, coaching, and recognition, not just evaluation. The trend is clearly towards more humane and effective approaches:

Continuous Feedback

Organisations are ditching the once-a-year review in favour of regular one-on-one check-ins. This allows feedback to be timely, forward-looking and less fraught. It's hard to overstate the relief employees feel when the dreaded annual appraisal is replaced by a normal conversation. One Deloitte study found only eight per cent of companies believed their performance management process was adding value.[6] No wonder a revolution is underway, and by 2015, 75 per cent of companies surveyed rated it an important issue to fix. Frequent feedback loops keep employees on track and show that the company is invested in their improvement continually, not just judging past mistakes.

Strength-Based Approach

Forward-thinking leaders encourage managers to recognise and build on strengths rather than obsess about weaknesses. Research shows people grow faster when coached in areas of strength; it boosts confidence and engagement, which then spills over into tackling weaker areas. A practical tip: some firms ask managers to write one or two key strength contributions for each team member every quarter and discuss how to leverage those. This doesn't mean ignoring problems, but it frames the conversation around potential ('How can we get even more of your best work?') rather than just shortcomings.

Peer Feedback and Recognition

Human-centred teams often democratise performance input. Tools like 360-degree feedback (gathering input from peers, subordinates, customers) paint a richer picture of someone's impact than a top-down review alone. Many companies also deploy social recognition platforms (e.g. Workhuman, Bonusly) where co-workers can thank each other publicly for good work. This fosters a positive performance culture where appreciation is frequent. In fact, a joint study by Workhuman and Gallup found that well-recognised employees were 45 per cent less likely to quit and reported significantly higher engagement.[7] Timely praise can be more motivating than any rating or small bonus.

Decoupling Performance from Pay

Some organisations separate the developmental feedback discussion from the compensation decision discussion. Why? Because the moment employees sense money is on the line, they become defensive or anxious, and the coaching aspect gets lost.[8] By having a growth-focused conversation first (no talk of salary or bonuses) and discussing raises or bonuses at a different time, managers can ensure the employee *hears* the feedback and ideas for growth.

When done right, employees actually look forward to performance chats as valuable for their career, rather than seeing them as a necessary evil tied to a pay negotiation.

Empowering teams means giving them a voice in decisions. Many companies use forums, councils, or pulse surveys to gather employee input on areas like customer service or workplace policies. For example, John Lewis involved frontline staff in redesigning its stores for the digital age. Employees in pilot stores tested new layouts, providing feedback on what improved sales and what didn't.[9]

This participatory approach sparked innovations leadership might not have envisioned, and it boosted employee morale. It aligns with the Agile principle of empowering those closest to the work to test and iterate, rather than relying on top-down plans.

Prioritising Well-Being and Flexibility

Work is not sustainable if it grinds people down. A truly human-centric workplace must actively support employees' well-being – physical, mental and emotional – and provide flexibility to balance work with life. In recent years, this has gone from a nice-to-have to a core strategic priority for leading organisations (turbo-charged by the pandemic, which laid bare how stress and burnout can explode if unchecked).

As one survey found, 92 per cent of workers say it's important that their employer supports mental health[10], and since COVID-19 about 81 per cent of workplaces increased their focus on employee mental health initiatives.[11] The logic is simple: healthy, happy employees are more engaged and productive (not to mention humanely, it's the right thing to do).

This section explores how companies are bolstering well-being, from novel wellness tech and programmes to flexible schedules and even rethinking the length of the working week. We'll also examine the growing movement to protect employees' personal time (the 'right to disconnect').

Organisations that will thrive are those that will move from programmes to a culture of care. Employee well-being has many facets: managing work stress, supporting mental health, encouraging physical fitness and fostering a general environment where people feel valued rather than expendable. Progressive employers approach this on multiple levels. Let's look at some of them below.

Wellness Programmes and Tech

Over the past decade, wellness benefits have surged, including mindfulness apps, yoga, step challenges, counselling hotlines, on-site gyms and more. But it's not just trendy perks; companies are getting strategic. Salesforce, for instance, offers monthly 'B-Well' mental health days and a retreat for employees to recharge. Many employers now provide digital therapeutics like Calm, Headspace, Woebot, or tele-therapy via Lyra Health. The need is real: in 2023, 77 per cent of employers saw a rise in mental health concerns.[12]

Workload and Burnout Prevention

Yoga won't help if workloads are unmanageable or deadlines relentless. Smart organisations address burnout at the root, hiring temp help during crunch times, training managers to spot overload and enforcing reasonable hours. Some European companies shut down email servers after hours to prevent 24/7 work creep. Volkswagen stops routing emails to phones 30 minutes after shifts end.[13] A UK ad firm created 'Quiet Fridays' with no meetings or client calls, letting staff catch up and sign off by 3 p.m. Such practices build healthier rhythms. The key is organisational norms that support well-being, not demanding heroic resilience just to survive the week.

Manager Training

Managers are the front line of well-being. Many firms now train them in basic mental health first aid, spotting signs like irritability, withdrawal or drops in performance, and responding with empathy and guidance. It's also about showing that compassion and high standards can coexist. One global bank introduced the COPE mnemonic: **Check in, Offer support, Prioritise workload, and Encourage**

time off. Teams with COPE-trained managers reported lower stress and maintained productivity. This proves that when managers support well-being, performance follows.

Inclusive Well-Being

Well-being initiatives must be inclusive. Needs vary. A young single employee may value social events, while a working parent may prefer flexible hours or childcare support. Fitness challenges might motivate some but alienate others. A menu of options and regular feedback help everyone find value. Inclusivity also means addressing specific challenges like assistive tech for differently abled staff or burnout among remote workers. Kenya's exploration of a Right to Disconnect law reflected the pressure remote workers feel to always be 'on'. In short, well-being must be tailored, not one-size-fits-all.

Flexibility and New Ways of Working

Hand-in-hand with well-being is the idea of flexibility, giving employees more control over *when, where, and how much* they work. Rigid nine-to-five office-bound models are fading in many industries, accelerated by the successful global experiment in remote work during the pandemic. What emerged is a strong employee desire for flexibility. A 2021 study of 5,000 workers found 77 per cent would prefer to work for a company that gives them the flexibility to work from anywhere, and 59 per cent said flexibility of location and hours is more important than salary.[14] That is huge. Moreover, 61 per cent would prefer to choose when to come into the office versus being told a fixed schedule. Employees, it seems, want to be treated as adults who can decide how best to meet their responsibilities.

Forward-looking organisations are accommodating this in various ways:

- **Hybrid Work**

    The dominant model today is hybrid – but what sets companies apart is who controls the schedule. Human-centric firms offer team or individual choice. Atlassian's 'Team Anywhere' lets staff live and work anywhere in countries where it operates, coming to the office only when needed. This expanded its talent pool and boosted satisfaction.[15]

    A 2022 Zoom survey found that 64 per cent of companies use hybrid setups and 75 per cent of leaders expect more changes ahead. Notably, 84 per cent cite higher productivity and 62 per cent better talent recruitment as reasons for flexibility.[16] But hybrid work has challenges – firms must invest in tech like video tools and digital whiteboards to ensure remote staff aren't sidelined. In fact, 72 per cent of employees said their company needs to improve tech for remote work. Smart firms are doing so. One London design firm even created a virtual water cooler and an always-on video kiosk named 'Bob' that remote staff could steer around the office, mixing humour and innovation to stay connected.

- **Flexible Hours**

    Flexibility is expanding beyond location to when work gets

done. Some companies use flexitime windows. E.g., required availability from 11 a.m. – 3 p.m., with the rest scheduled freely. Others offer condensed weeks like longer days Monday–Thursday and Friday afternoons off. Results-Only Work Environments (ROWE), first tried at Best Buy, focus on outcomes, not hours.[17] One pilot participant called it 'life-changing', gaining freedom to manage her time while improving performance. Teams in ROWE took ownership of goals and thrived. The key: clear communication, as most teams set overlap hours or use shared calendars to stay aligned.

- **Compressed Working Weeks and the Four-Day Week**
  One of the most talked-about flexibility trends is the four-day working week. Iceland's large trial (2015–2019) with 2,500 workers showed no drop in productivity – sometimes even gains, and major improvements in well-being, including reduced stress and burnout.[18] Researchers called it an 'overwhelming success,' and now 86 per cent of Iceland's workforce has the right to shorter hours. Inspired by this, trials have followed in New Zealand, Japan, Spain, the UK and more. Microsoft Japan saw a 40 per cent productivity boost in its 2019 trial.[19] A 2022 UK pilot with 70 companies and 3,300 workers found reduced stress, no loss in output, and even revenue increases; 90 per cent kept the new schedule.[20]
  The four-day week encourages smarter work, fewer meetings, focus, and better time use. It may not suit every industry, but even partial steps like meeting-free days or six-hour workdays

can deliver benefits. The core lesson: redesigning the working week for well-being can also enhance performance – a true win-win.

- **Leave and Time-Off Policies**
 Flexible, humane workplaces are rethinking leave policies. Generous parental leave for all parents, not just mothers, is one example, along with sabbaticals to recharge or pursue personal growth. Some companies have adopted unlimited holiday policies, though these can backfire if not supported by a culture that encourages taking time off. For instance, some companies with unlimited PTO saw employees taking less time off, fearing it might reflect poorly on them, leading to 'minimums' or mandated holiday days.
 The core idea is to treat employees as whole people with lives outside of work. Netflix, for example, emphasises results over hours worked or holiday time.[21] Many European companies also shut down for a few weeks in the summer to encourage recharging. These policies convey that rest is valued, not viewed as a lack of commitment – a message that's especially important in today's always-connected world.

- **Employee Choice and Voice in Flexibility**
 In rolling out flexibility, a wise strategy is to let teams customise what works for them. Top-down mandates (e.g. 'all staff back to the office three days a week') can breed resentment or simply not suit certain roles. We saw a vivid ex-

ample when Apple's management announced a mandatory three-days-in-office policy: employees pushed back in an open letter, imploring that 'remote and location-flexible work decisions be as autonomous for a team to decide as are hiring decisions.'[22] They basically asked Apple to trust each team to figure out the right balance.

- **The Right to Disconnect and Work-Life Boundaries**
A challenge in our hyper-connected world is ensuring that flexibility doesn't lead to work seeping into all hours. With laptops always within reach, many struggle to disconnect. This has led to the 'Right to Disconnect' movement, starting in Europe with France's 2017 law, protecting workers' personal time by allowing them to ignore emails outside working hours.[23] Since then, at least 11 European Union (EU) countries, including Spain, Ireland, and Italy, have introduced similar regulations. For employers, adopting such policies, whether required by law or not, promotes a healthier work-life balance.

Some companies have creatively encouraged disconnection, like a Canadian marketing firm adding a line to after-hours emails: 'The sender of this email does not expect a response outside your working hours.' Others use email scheduling, letting employees draft emails late but send them during business hours. Ultimately, a performance culture that respects boundaries tends to get better sustained performance. People return recharged rather than running on fumes. One humorous example: a consultancy in Sweden had a big sign in the office, 'Go Home!' At 5 p.m., it would flash. It became a playful symbol of their work-hard-then-stop-hard ethos. They found it improved client deliverables because consultants came in the next day with fresh minds instead of grinding late with diminishing returns. As the joke goes, 'Are you working hard, or hardly working?' The goal is to work smart, then rest well.

Flexibility and well-being are about treating employees as responsible adults with whole lives. When you give them flexibility, most will repay the trust with dedication. And when you support their well-being, they'll have the capacity to give their best. Gone are the days when stoic endurance of stress was a badge of honour. In the future of work, balance is the new productivity.

The Chief Human Strategist (CHS): A Must-Have for Future-Forward Organisations

As artificial intelligence continues to reshape the business landscape, a new leadership role is emerging, one that will determine whether organisations thrive or merely survive in the age of intelligent machines. This is the role of the Chief Human Strategist. The CHS will be the executive guardian of humanity within technology-driven enterprises. Unlike traditional HR or technology leaders, the CHS will operate at the intersection of human potential, ethics, and strategic growth. Their mission? To ensure that technology amplifies rather than replaces the human advantage.

The Chief Human Strategist will:
1. Integrate AI responsibly, ensuring it augments human capability and protects organisational values.

2. Anticipate and shape workforce evolution, building cultures where continuous learning and adaptability are the norm.

3. Embed ethics and trust at the core of innovation, safeguarding dignity and fairness in every decision.

4. Leverage inclusion and belonging as engines of creativity, resilience, and performance.

5. Champion the irreplaceable edge – empathy, creativity, and critical thinking as the ultimate differentiators of success.

In the years ahead, companies that appoint visionary CHS will not only navigate disruption more effectively, they will set the standard for what it means to lead with purpose in an AI powered world. In the future of work, the CHS will be the voice ensuring that humanity remains the ultimate competitive advantage.

Gone are the days when stoic endurance of stress was a badge of honour. In the future of work, balance is the new productivity.

11

Time Together: An Informa Case Study

In an era where remote work has become the norm and digital connectivity often replaces face-to-face interaction, organisations worldwide are facing a crucial question: how do we balance flexibility with the undeniable power of human connection?

At its core, Time Together is more than just a corporate directive; it's a commitment to human interaction, career growth, and cultural agility. It's about recognising that while technology can bridge gaps, it cannot replace the depth of relationships, the spontaneity of innovation and the trust that is built when people are physically present.

In a world that often prioritises efficiency over engagement, Informa is choosing to prioritise both. This is an example of how business decisions and people's priorities intersect: active listening, adaptability, and cultural intelligence.

Stephen Carter, Group CEO of Informa, captures this philosophy powerfully:

'As we expand and grow in new markets and countries and cultures and as we accelerate career and opportunity mobility, we need to be as diverse and culturally agile as we are ambitious for growth.'

Why Time Together Matters

The post-pandemic workplace has given us a paradox. While hybrid and remote work have created flexibility, they have also led to decreased collaboration, weaker team cohesion, and diluted workplace culture. Research from McKinsey and Harvard Business Review shows that:[1]

- Companies that prioritise in-person collaboration see 20–25 per cent higher innovation rates.

- Employee satisfaction is 30 per cent higher in workplaces where teams regularly meet in person.

Face-to-face interactions lead to stronger mentorship, career development, and leadership visibility. At Informa, Time Together is designed to address these realities. The strategy is built on five pillars of human connection:

1. **Time together in person as teams**: fostering collaboration, planning, and innovation.

2. **Time together with customers, partners, and industry leaders:** building deeper relationships and understanding market needs.

3. **Time together at live events:** engaging in real-time knowledge exchange and networking.

4. **Time together in shared workplaces:** making full use of

world-class office spaces that drive productivity and belonging.

5. **Time together to create career growth:** ensuring that opportunities for mentorship, learning, and leadership visibility remain strong.

Time Together is not about forcing people back into the office; it's about ensuring that Informa's people are set up for growth, opportunity and long-term success.

Beyond the Desk: Human Connection as a Business Strategy

One of the most overlooked consequences of remote work is the loss of social capital, the intangible but critical connections that fuel trust, collaboration, and mentorship. Before the pandemic, people formed these relationships organically through coffee chats, hallway conversations, and spontaneous brainstorming sessions. Now, they require deliberate effort. Time Together is a strategic response to some of these challenges. By embedding in-person collaboration into Informa's operating model, the company is ensuring that new ideas flow freely; mentorship happens naturally; and culture remains strong. A 2023 study by the Harvard Business School found that teams working primarily in-person were more likely to generate breakthrough ideas, mentor junior colleagues effectively and build stronger long-term relationships compared to fully remote teams.[2] Informa is aligning with these findings by ensuring that time together isn't just a return to tradition; it's a leap towards a more engaged, connected, and innovative future.

Career Mobility and the Visibility Imperative

One of the most compelling aspects of the Time Together strategy is its commitment to internal career mobility. At a recent Leadership Summit, Informa set an ambitious target: at least 50 per cent of new roles should be filled internally. This is a game-changer! In many organisations, the 'out of sight, out of mind' problem has widened since remote work became prevalent. Employees who are not physically present often miss out on career opportunities, leadership visibility, and professional networking. By increasing in-person engagement, Informa is ensuring that colleagues gain greater access to mentorship and sponsorship opportunities, while leaders are better positioned to recognise and promote talent from within. This approach makes career mobility not merely a concept but a deliberate and strategic outcome. The message is clear: visibility and connection foster opportunity.

Cultural Agility

As a multinational organisation, Informa operates in diverse markets across different cultures, languages, and business environments. The ability to adapt, understand, and respect these differences is critical for success.

In-person engagement plays a key role here. Time Together enables:
- Stronger cross-cultural collaboration

- Deeper understanding of customer and partner needs.
- Real-time knowledge exchange in global markets.

In China, India, and the Middle East, business relationships are built on trust, personal interactions and face-to-face meetings, a cultural expectation that remote communication cannot fully replace. Informa's investment in physical office spaces worldwide demonstrates its long-term commitment to these markets.

'If the world is a shared village, our job is to understand and respect its customs and cultures where we choose to operate.'
—Stephen Carter.

By embedding time together as a core strategy, Informa is ensuring that its workforce is not just working in different countries but truly operating as a globally connected organisation.

The Human Advantage of Time Together

In a world increasingly shaped by AI, automation, and digital connectivity, human connection remains the most valuable competitive edge.

Technology accelerates work, but human relationships accelerate growth. Efficiency drives output, but collaboration drives innovation. Remote work provides flexibility, but in-person work creates opportunity.

Finding the Balance

Time Together represents an important evolution in how businesses approach collaboration, engagement, and performance.

It's a necessary strategy. But like all change, it must be implemented with agility, emotional intelligence, and inclusion at its core. Workplace transformation is never just about logistics; it's about people.

The future of work isn't about remote vs. in-office; it's about creating environments where people thrive, where collaboration fuels success and where inclusion is not an afterthought, but a foundation.

By embedding Time Together into its core business strategy, Informa is making a bold statement: The future of work isn't just about where we work; it's about how we grow, connect and succeed together. Ultimately, our greatest advantage is one another – being together, connecting, and collaborating in ways no technology can replicate. And that is what will set the best companies apart in the years to come.

Embracing the AI Time Dividend

As we stand at the intersection of human brilliance and machine learning, the future belongs not to those who resist this change, but to those who adapt purposefully. Across industries, AI is no longer a distant concept; it's a present and evolving reality. From ChatGPT to Copilot, Gemini to Claude, many of us are already engaging with AI tools to varying degrees.

At Informa, this transformation is being brought even closer to home through **Elysia**, our own purpose-built AI assistant. More than just a support agent, Elysia represents a new era of human-AI collaboration, designed by Informa for Informa. It's a shared capability that connects colleagues across teams, brands, functions, and regions under a single digital network of learning and enablement. What makes this moment significant is not only the tool itself, but the clarity of direction.

Spending time with and on Elysia every day is the call to action, and it is not rooted in fear of obsolescence, but in the opportunity of augmentation. Elysia has been launched as part of the 2025–2028 One Informa Programme, and it embodies everything *The Human Advantage* stands for, using technology to elevate our uniquely human skills: creativity, empathy, critical thinking, and collaboration.

Just as the company once responded to the global disruption of the pandemic with decisive care, ensuring remote work, safeguarding jobs and reimagining events, this moment marks another pivot. But this time, the instruction isn't to pull back – it's to lean in, to experiment, to prompt better and create smarter.

Elysia invites us to reimagine how we:

- Draft, edit and co-create content

- Analyse data and gain sharper insights

- Plan budgets, product roadmaps, and events

- Capture meeting notes and summarise outcomes

- Research, code and ideate

- Engage with customers and build better solutions

In doing so, we unlock what the Group CEO, Stephen Carter aptly refers to as the **AI Time Dividend**; the surplus time and capacity we gain by working more efficiently through AI. Imagine what becomes possible if we each became 20 per cent more creative, informed, productive and/or responsive. That's a full working day each week to re-invest in what truly matters: deeper thinking, stronger human-centred relationships, better service, more impact.

The real message? Elysia is not here to replace Informa staff; it is here to *release* them, to free them from the mechanical, so they can spend more time in the meaningful. It gives them the edge, not because it makes them less human, but because it makes their humanity more potent.

Let this be a reminder; the tools may be artificial, but the advantage remains deeply human.

'Use your time to do more valuable things – don't be fearful – do what only you can do better. Leave the process drudgery to automation.' Inspired by Stephen Carter.

In a world that often prioritises efficiency over engagement, Informa is choosing to prioritise both.

12

BUILDING PSYCHOLOGICAL RESILIENCE

Having the right mindset and agility sets the stage, but resilience also involves emotional strength and coping strategies. Life will throw curveballs, from job losses and business failures to personal tragedies or health crises. Psychological resilience helps you handle stress and adversity healthily, maintaining your well-being and motivation.

Social Support and Relationships

It might sound soft for a business context, but never underestimate the power of human connection in resilience.[1] Whether it's friends, family, mentors, colleagues, or a support group, having people you trust and can talk to will bolster you in tough times. Knowing you're not alone while facing a challenge makes it more manageable.

On the flip side, resilient individuals also *seek* support, are not afraid to reach out and say, 'I'm struggling with this, can we talk?' or 'Can you help me brainstorm solutions?' This proactive use of your social network is a resilience strategy in itself. So, one practical tip: nurture your relationships. They are both a safety net and a springboard. Teams that foster empathy and mutual support will also find this pays off when collective stress hits. In personal terms, staying connected, whether via regular catch-ups, networking or even humorous chats that lighten the mood, can be your emotional ballast.

Physical Well-Being and Resilience

Body and mind are tightly linked. It's immensely harder to be mentally resilient when you're sleep-deprived, malnourished or physically unwell. Prioritising sleep, exercise, and a decent diet can significantly improve your capacity to handle stress. Exercise in particular is often called nature's antidepressant; it releases endorphins and can improve mood and cognitive function.

Think of physical self-care as maintaining the vehicle (your body) that carries your brain and heart through challenges. You wouldn't embark on a long, bumpy road trip with flat tires and no fuel, right? Facing life's bumpy rides is easier when your tires (health) are pumped and your tank (energy) is filled. Many leadership development programmes now incorporate wellness and resilience coaching that cover sleep and stress management, recognising that high performance isn't just about skills or IQ, but also about stamina and balance.

Goal Flexibility: Knowing Your 'Why'

Resilience also comes from having a sense of purpose or a 'why' that motivates you, but being flexible about the 'how'. For example, if your core purpose is to educate others and a classroom teaching job is no longer viable, a resilient mindset would seek other avenues to fulfil that purpose – perhaps via online tutoring, writing a blog or working in corporate training.

Anchoring to a purpose gives you direction (an essential during turbulent times, to avoid feeling lost), but flexibility ensures you don't cling to one job or identity. This combination of determination and adaptability is often seen in resilient people; they're persistent in *goal pursuit* but also quick to adapt the path as needed.

Emotional Tone

It's worth noting that building resilience doesn't mean you have to be relentlessly cheerful or in denial of pain. In fact, resilient people do feel the sadness, anger, or grief of setbacks; they just don't get permanently stuck there. They acknowledge the emotions ('this hurts, I feel frustrated'), perhaps even use them as fuel for change, and then gradually move forward. It's perfectly human (and healthy) to allow yourself a bad day or a good cry when things go wrong. Emotional authenticity can coexist with resilience. The key is that after processing emotions, resilient individuals find ways to regroup and not let the negative emotion become their permanent soundtrack.

Reinvention Practices for Individuals

Now that we've covered mindset, agility, and emotional coping, let's talk *action*. How can individuals proactively reinvent themselves?

What practical steps turn the abstract idea of 'reinvention' into reality? Here are some strategies and exercises used in coaching and personal development that help translate resilience into reinvention:

Odyssey Planning (Design Your Life Approach)

Have you ever struggled to decide your next move in life or work? Odyssey Planning, from Stanford's *Designing Your Life* programme, helps by treating life planning like design prototyping.[2] You imagine three possible future lives (5–10 years ahead) – like 'Become a Freelance Consultant,' 'Go back to university,' or 'Turn my side hobby into a business.' For each, you map out what it involves: its pros and cons, timeline, and how it fits your values. Then you prototype: run small experiments to test these paths before committing. That might mean shadowing a consultant, taking a night class, or selling your hobby product at a weekend market.

Reinvention Sprints

Taking a cue from the tech world's 'design sprints' and hackathons, some individuals (and companies) are using short intense bursts of focus to drive reinvention. A *reinvention sprint* might be, for instance, a dedicated four-week programme you create for yourself to pursue a new skill or project wholeheartedly and see what comes of it. There's even a recent coaching programme dubbed 'The Reinvention Sprint' that guides professionals through a four-week process to 'hit reset, focus on what matters, and take action – without overwhelm'.[3] The idea here is to give yourself permission to pause your routine and deeply engage with change, essentially scheduling reinvention.

Future-Proofing Your Skills and Micro-Learning

In a practical vein, personal reinvention often involves updating one's skills. This doesn't always mean a complete career about-face or going back to school for three years. Many people stay in the same general field but reinvent *how* they work or *what* they focus on. Thanks to the abundance of online courses and micro-learning platforms, you can continuously reskill and upskill yourself. For example, a marketing professional might take a course in data analytics to reinvent herself as a data-driven marketer; a schoolteacher might learn coding on the side and eventually move into educational technology roles.

Narrative Reinvention: Rewriting Your Story

Narrative therapy, used by psychologists and coaches, involves rewriting your life or career story to highlight resilience and growth. Why? Because the way we tell our story shapes how we see ourselves. A narrative like 'I had bad luck' is disempowering, while 'I overcame X and learnt Y' restores agency.

In the face of a layoff, one version says, 'I wasn't good enough,' the other, 'It pushed me to grow.' Both may be true, but only one moves you forward.

Reinvention at the Organisational Level: Building Agile and Adaptive Teams

If individuals need resilience and reinvention to thrive, organisations – which are collections of individuals – need it *exponentially*. A new technology can upend industries overnight, consumer preferences can shift like the wind, and global events (a pandemic, anyone?) can force businesses to change nearly everything about how they operate.

Let's begin with some stories because nothing drives the point home better than seeing reinvention live and in colour.

Case Study: Fiskars (Finland)

Fiskars, Finland's oldest company (founded in 1649), is a masterclass in staying relevant.[4] Known today for its iconic orange-handled scissors, Fiskars began as a local ironworks and has continually reinvented itself through industrial revolutions, world wars, and the digital era. In recent decades, it brought in bold leadership and made strategic acquisitions like design brands Iittala and the Wedgwood, Waterford, Royal Doulton (WWRD) group to stay ahead of consumer trends.

As CEO Teemu Kangas-Kärki noted, Fiskars survives because it embraces transformation. Rather than clinging to legacy products, it asks, 'What's next?' Reinvention is a mindset woven into its culture. Internally, they remind each other: people often overestimate short-term change and underestimate long-term impact – wisdom any organisation can use when navigating turbulence while playing the long game.

Case Study: LEGO (Denmark)

LEGO's near-collapse in the early 2000s reads like a dramatic novel with a happy ending.[5] After decades of success, the company over-diversified into theme parks, video games, and dolls, losing focus. By 2003, sales had dropped 30 per cent, debt hit $800 million, and an internal report declared LEGO hadn't added value in a decade. New CEO Jørgen Vig Knudstorp called it 'a burning platform... likely won't survive.'

What followed was a masterclass in reinvention. LEGO returned to its core: the brick and its community – kids and Adult Fans of LEGO (AFOLs). It cut underperforming projects, embraced user co-creation (LEGO Ideas), secured smart licences and expanded into media that aligned with its brand. By 2015, LEGO had become the world's most powerful brand, with profits soaring and at times outpacing even Apple. The key? Resilience through tough self-assessment, rediscovery of purpose and bold innovation. Knudstorp honoured LEGO's heritage while leading change, proving that reinvention is possible, even from the brink.

Despite the differences in these case studies, common threads emerge: proactive change, agility, learning from setbacks and a people-centric approach. None of these reinventions was easy. All involved risk, learning, and rallying the troops around a new way of doing things. In the following sections, we'll distil strategies and frameworks that can help organisations cultivate this kind of resilience and reinvention capacity more systematically.

Fostering a Resilient Culture: Leadership and Team Dynamics

If you peel back the layers of any successful organisational reinvention, you often find a culture that enabled it. *Culture* can sound abstract, but in essence, it's 'how we do things here' – the norms, values, and behaviours that are encouraged (or discouraged). To thrive in a changing world, an organisation's culture should encourage adaptability, learning, and shared purpose. Here are some key aspects of a resilient, change-ready culture:

Psychological Safety: The Foundation of Adaptive Teams

Google's Project Aristotle found that the top factor in team effectiveness is psychological safety, a work environment where people feel safe to take risks, ask for help or admit mistakes without fear.[6] This is crucial for reinvention, since innovation involves risk and failure. Without psychological safety, teams hide problems and hold back ideas that could lead to breakthroughs. It's been linked to higher innovation, better error prevention and faster adaptation. As Harvard's Amy Edmondson explains, it's a climate of candour, trust, and respect.[7] Leaders can foster it by being approachable, owning their fallibility and encouraging input, even imperfect ideas. A little humour helps too. The result? A fearless team ready to challenge norms and drive change.

Learning Culture in Organisations

Just as individuals thrive with a growth mindset, organisations benefit from a learning culture, one that encourages learning at all levels, from training to informal knowledge sharing and experimental pilots. They treat mistakes as learning opportunities, not failures. Tech firms like Amazon and Toyota use 'blameless post-mortems' to examine errors without blame, aiming to improve systems and avoid repeat issues.

Learning cultures also invest in people. American Telephone and Telegraph (AT&T), for example, retrained its workforce in coding and data science to stay relevant. Even smaller firms can promote learning through mentorships, lunch-and-learns, or project time like Google's '20 per cent time', which led to Gmail. The result was a workforce better equipped for change. One Deloitte study found that such cultures are 92 per cent more likely to create innovative products, giving them a clear edge in reinvention.[8]

Empowerment and Decentralised Decision-Making

In fast-changing times, speed is critical, especially as rigid hierarchies slow organisations down. Resilient companies empower teams to make domain-level decisions, guided by clear principles. Take China's Haier Group: it broke itself into self-managing, micro-entrepreneurial teams, giving frontline units autonomy to pivot and innovate. This 'platform' model keeps Haier agile in a dynamic market.[9]

Not every company needs such a radical shift, but the core idea applies: push authority to where the information is. Frontline workers often spot change first. Empowering them to act speeds response, boosts morale and strengthens ownership. Without it, decisions lag and opportunities slip away.

Unified Purpose and Vision (The North Star)

In turbulent times, a clear sense of purpose serves as a lighthouse, guiding and grounding teams amid constant change. Sasol's 'One Sasol' initiative embodies this principle[10] and IBM's 1990s reinvention under Lou Gerstner shows how shared purpose can guide massive transformation.[11] Gerstner rallied IBM around becoming an end-to-end solutions provider, shedding old businesses, retraining staff and acquiring new capabilities, all aligned with a renewed mission to better serve customers.

Purpose gives change emotional resonance and helps align global teams. Reiterating 'why we exist' helps people make sense of the hard work and stay motivated. Even if strategy shifts, a strong purpose, like a renewable energy startup aiming to power communities and help the planet, keeps teams focused and inspired.

Celebrating Reinvention Stories

Stories and symbols reinforce culture. Organisations that value reinvention will hold up examples of it from within as inspiration. Did a team in the Brazil office find a clever new business model? Make it a case study to share company-wide. Did an employee radically reskill and move from one department to another, adding immense value as a result? Recognise and celebrate that journey. These stories become part of the lore that signals to everyone: *change is not just accepted here; it's celebrated.* Some companies even have 'failure awards,' a light-hearted prize for a bold experiment that failed, to underline that taking risks is valued. This kind of positive reinforcement is vital. It's one thing to say 'innovate, please!' in a mission statement, but when employees see colleagues actually being rewarded and recognised for innovative efforts (even those that flop), they truly believe it's safe to try. As a humorous example, Tata Group in India has a 'Dare To Try' award for the most audacious failure, thus turning the fear of failure on its head.[12] The result? A cultural permission to attempt reinvention without fearing career suicide if it doesn't pan out the first time.

Psychological resilience helps you handle stress and adversity healthily, maintaining your well-being and motivation.

13

Leveraging Technology

Technology often overwhelms us at work and in most places. We've all felt it: the relentless flood of emails, endless app notifications, and that nagging sense that we're always 'on'. However, when used thoughtfully, tech and digital tools can support human-centred workplaces, enhancing well-being, inclusion and collaboration rather than causing overload.

I'll admit it; technology used to intimidate me. The constant pings, notifications, and seemingly endless array of apps can feel overwhelming. Yet, in recent times, I've discovered something vital: when we thoughtfully integrate technology into our daily routine, it doesn't have to drain our energy or distract us. Instead, it can uplift, empower, and connect us in deeply human ways.

Workplace design, both physical and digital, should prioritise comfort, safety, and inclusivity; what I call; AI inclusion and digital inclusion.

AI Inclusion

AI inclusion is about ensuring that artificial intelligence is designed and deployed with equity and fairness at its core. It means intentionally embedding diverse human and cultural perspectives into AI systems, actively mitigating biases, and using AI to amplify rather than limit human potential. A future where technology supports inclusive leadership, cultural intelligence, and empowers everyone, regardless of background, to thrive in the digital age.

Digital Inclusion

Digital inclusion refers to creating equitable access and meaningful participation in the digital world. It encompasses breaking down barriers related to accessibility, affordability, digital skills, and representation to ensure no one is left behind. It's a strategic commitment to fostering human-centric communities and workplaces where technology serves as a bridge, enabling everyone to contribute fully and benefit from our increasingly connected society.

Well-Being Tech and Data Insights

An exciting frontier is using data and analytics to promote well-being without invading privacy. Microsoft's Viva Insights tool analyses email and calendar data, spots trends like meeting overload or after-hours work spikes, encouraging healthier habits. This led Microsoft managers to reduce double-booking and establish 'no internal meeting' days, promoting work-life balance. Similarly, companies use pulse surveys (e.g., Culture Amp, Glint) to regularly assess stress and morale, allowing leaders to act quickly. Some offer wearables or apps that track health metrics and reward healthy behaviours.

British Petroleum's (BP) Fitbit challenges saw employees walking millions of steps and reporting better fitness. An excellent example of this human-centred ethos is Informa's 'Walk The World' (WTW), an annual global event designed to foster genuine human connections. Each year, colleagues from across the world come together physically and virtually, walking side by side to celebrate well-being, community, and the enduring power of face-to-face interaction. WTW is a reminder that authentic human connections remain essential for nurturing inclusive cultures and driving meaningful engagement.

Inclusive Design Tools

Technology increasingly serves as a powerful enabler for inclusivity, levelling the playing field and transforming how people participate and contribute.

Microsoft Teams Accessibility Features

Live captioning, transcription, and speaker attribution help participants who are deaf, hard-of-hearing, non-native speakers, or working in noisy environments.[1] Features like background noise reduction, translation of captions, keyboard navigation, and screen reader compatibility further enhance accessibility.

Inclusive Authoring Tools

Tools like Textio analyse job postings in real time to flag gendered or exclusionary language. Companies have reported faster hiring cycles and significantly more diverse applicant pools by adjusting tone and terminology.[2] Inclusive design goes beyond accessibility; it anticipates diverse needs in how information is designed, delivered, and received.

Emotion-Aware AR Captions in Education

A new AR interface enriches live captioning by overlaying emotional context (e.g., tone, gestures) in STEM classrooms, helping deaf or neurodiverse learners interpret nuance in real-time lecture settings.[3]

Inclusive AI and Learning Platforms

AI-driven learning and collaboration platforms can help close opportunity gaps by offering personalised course recommendations – with some platforms now nudging underrepresented groups towards leadership or technical development programmes. One organisation saw gender balance improve significantly after AI began recommending a tech leadership programme to high-performing women – resulting in a notable boost in female applications.

Physical Space Design with Humans in Mind

Even in hybrid settings, thoughtful design matters. Flexible layouts combine quiet zones, breakout areas, standing desks, lounges, and biophilic elements to support focus and well-being. Steelcase, for example, used sensor data to redesign space utilisation and found stand-up meeting zones increased collaboration. Phone booths, quiet pods, CO_2 monitors, and ergonomically adjustable desks and lighting help individuals regulate sensory input and comfort. Incorporating air quality and lighting ensures the environment adapts to diverse needs.

Pixar's campus features a central atrium with a cereal bar and mail sorting room designed to spark spontaneous interactions. This casual, playful space reduces hierarchy and encourages creativity, showing the value of designing for human connection, not just function.

Why Inclusive Design Leads to the Human Advantage

By embedding accessible, inclusive options, whether through tech, physical space, or policy, organisations unlock:

Equitable participation – everyone, regardless of ability, background, or language, can contribute meaningfully.

Diverse representation – more varied perspectives enrich creativity, decision-making and innovation.

Psychological safety – when structures adapt to the individual, people feel seen, valued and safe to bring their full selves.

Cutting-Edge: Virtual Reality, Augmented Reality and Virtual Collaboration Spaces

Virtual reality (VR) and augmented reality (AR) are transforming how we work, offering immersive ways to support human-centred objectives, especially in remote or distributed environments. For example, Accenture took a bold step in 2021 by purchasing 60,000 Oculus VR headsets to onboard new employees.[4] They created a virtual campus called the 'Nth Floor,' allowing remote hires to meet avatars of colleagues, attend training, and even have casual coffee chats – replicating the in-person onboarding experience. This initiative has seen over 150,000 employees engage with the VR environment, resulting in higher excitement and connection among new hires compared to traditional video calls.

AR is also making an impact in training and maintenance by overlaying digital information on the real world. In one case, AR glasses guided factory technicians step by step through repairs, reducing error and speeding up skill acquisition. A company in Japan used AR for on-the-job training, enabling junior engineers to follow AR prompts while supervisors remotely provided guidance.[5] This allowed mentorship at scale without physical proximity, empowering junior staff, and boosting confidence.

Even for everyday collaboration, some teams are exploring persistent virtual spaces, like 3D virtual offices where avatars gather around a whiteboard. Though still emerging, these tools can make brainstorming sessions more engaging than traditional video calls. The key is using these tools only when they add value and respecting individual preferences. Some might still prefer a straightforward audio call.

Policy Innovation and the Future

Policy innovation plays a key role in designing a human-centred future. Beyond flexible work arrangements and the right-to-disconnect laws, some companies have gone further by advocating broader policy changes that support their employees. For example, some firms are championing better childcare infrastructure, which directly benefits their workforce. Other progressive policies include 'caretaker leave', which allows employees to take time off to care for elderly parents or sick family members. These policies may go beyond legal requirements but signal an organisation's values and set an example for others to follow.

At the global level, governments and businesses often influence one another. New Zealand, for example, introduced a Well-being Budget that reallocated spending towards mental health, family violence prevention, and child wellness.[6] This human-centred approach has gradually shaped workplace ethos, particularly in countries where such policies gain political traction. In Japan, dealing with issues of 'karōshi' (death by overwork), the government has encouraged initiatives like 'Premium Fridays' (allowing employees to leave early on the last Friday of the month) to reduce burnout.[7] Though slow, these changes highlight the growing recognition of the human cost of overwork. Similarly, some French companies pioneered 'right-to-disconnect' policies even before they became law, setting a positive precedent for the public sector.

In the end, the intersection of technology, workspace design and policy is all about creating an ecosystem where people can thrive. In this context, innovation isn't about the latest tech for tech's sake but about fostering healthier, more inclusive and empowering work environments. A humorous tech anecdote to end with: when an AI was asked how to make workplaces more human, it replied, 'By treating people like people, not robots.' A simple yet wise observation, and it didn't even need a neural network to figure that out!

The Human Advantage: Putting People First to Shape the Future

Across strategies, from leadership and culture to well-being, autonomy, and tech, a common thread emerges; humanity is the heart of a thriving workplace. When we design the future of work around humans, we unlock what we might call 'the human advantage' – the unique innovation, resilience, and passion people bring when they feel empowered, appreciated, and safe. This advantage is hard to replicate, as it stems from aligning organisational purpose with human values.

Consider the examples we have highlighted through this lens: In Spain, Panelfisa shifted from a traditional factory to a cooperative model, empowering individuals to grow stronger through economic challenges.[8] In Kenya, Safaricom's focus on inclusion and wellness drove innovation in mobile health and finance products, created by employees who deeply understand their diverse customers. In China, Haier shattered corporate norms, fostering an entrepreneurial spirit among its employees.[9] National work-time experiments in Iceland show that improving citizens' quality of life can boost productivity, challenging industrial-era work assumptions.[10]

Leaders reading this may wonder where to start, and the answer is simple: start from where you are, start now, and involve your people in the journey. Begin with a small pilot, like testing a new flexibility arrangement or feedback system in one department, and learn from it. Show that continuous improvement for your people is a priority. Some changes are large, like re-architecting an organisation, while others are small tweaks, like a regular team health check or revising a restrictive policy. Each step builds trust and shows employees they are valued.

Human-centred doesn't mean no rules or accountability. It's about achieving discipline through motivation, not fear. Shifting from external control to internal drive leads to more accountability. HCL Tech is a prime example. When employees were trusted, they took responsibility and thrived. Similarly, a small team with autonomy often exceeds expectations, putting in extra effort willingly.

Sustaining these efforts is key. Culture change is ongoing. Companies must keep listening, adapting and training new managers in the philosophy. Setbacks will occur, but leaders can acknowledge them, course-correct and reinforce commitment. As Rich Sheridan, CEO of Menlo Innovations says, 'It's not about being perfect; it's about catching ourselves when we're not and having mechanisms to fix it'.[11]

At Menlo, radical transparency keeps them honest, and while not everyone will adopt this approach, the principle of accountability to the culture is powerful.

Sustaining a human-centred environment also means measuring what truly matters. While traditional KPIs like sales and profit remain important, they should be balanced with metrics, such as employee engagement, well-being, retention rates, internal mobility, and inclusion.

The adage 'what gets measured gets managed' is key – if leadership talks about caring for people but only measures financial output, the internal message becomes unclear. Many companies now include people metrics in management dashboards, and some tie leader bonuses to engagement or diversity improvements. For example, when Marks & Spencer launched its transformation, the CEO made customer satisfaction and employee engagement as important as financial metrics, recognising that happy employees lead to happy customers.[12]

Celebrating success stories is another way to sustain a human-centred environment. Sharing stories about empowered teams or employees' suggestions leading to improvements creates emotional connections and reinforces the culture. Stories like those of Panelfisa can spark ideas within your own company and remind us that the goal is not just productivity, but human dignity and joy at work.

Humour also plays a vital role. In a human-centred workplace, laughter is not unprofessional but a sign of a healthy team. Whether it's an inside joke or a quirky team mascot, these moments of levity strengthen relationships and make work more enjoyable. When people say, 'I love my job', it's often because of the people and the joyful moments, not just the work itself.

Designing the future of work around humans is both a strategic imperative and a deeply optimistic endeavour. Even as machines get smarter, human creativity, empathy, and ingenuity remain the true advantage, flourishing only in the right conditions. By reshaping workplaces to empower people, organisations unlock previously inaccessible wells of performance and innovation.

We've explored global examples and practical tactics, but now it's up to each leader, team, and reader to carry this forward. It could begin with a simple question in your next meeting: 'What can we do to make our work more human-friendly?' Don't be surprised if the room fills with ideas. People are eager for this. The future isn't something that just happens to us; we design it. So, let's create a future of work where Monday mornings are met with energy (and maybe even a smile), workplaces buzz with trust and creativity and businesses and people thrive together.

Companies that embrace this will find that when humans are at the centre, performance, and profit naturally follow. More importantly, they'll leave a legacy – workplaces that empower people to become the best versions of themselves. That's the human advantage in full bloom, not man versus machine, but humanity unleashed to dream, create, care, and thrive.

As we stand on the cusp of an AI-driven future, one thing is clear: our uniquely human strengths will remain our greatest advantage.

Conclusion

In a world buzzing with AI and automation, it's easy to wonder what will set humans apart in the years ahead. Throughout this book, we've seen that the answer lies in timeless human qualities: empathy, emotional intelligence, creativity, resilience, adaptability, inclusion, and critical thinking. These traits have been the driving force behind effective leadership, vibrant workplace cultures, personal well-being, breakthrough innovation, and inclusive growth. Now, as we stand on the cusp of an AI-driven future, one thing is clear: our uniquely human strengths will remain our greatest advantage.

A Future Fuelled by Human Qualities

Far from rendering people obsolete, technology is making human skills *more* essential. Yes, AI is revolutionising work by automating routine tasks and crunching data, but AI alone isn't enough.[1] Machines excel at algorithms and efficiency, but they lack a heart and conscience. As experts note, AI struggles with emotional intelligence, creativity, and moral judgement, areas where human insight is irreplaceable. In fact, the more AI we deploy, the more we rely on what makes us human. New research reveals that 83 per cent of people believe AI will make uniquely human skills even **more** critical, and 76 per cent of employees 'crave more human connection' as AI use grows.[2] This points to a future where who we are matters more than ever.

Rather than a competition, imagine a powerful partnership: AI handling the grunt work while human empathy, creativity, and wisdom guide the way. This synergy, a true human-machine symbiosis – ensures that human ingenuity remains at the forefront of progress.[3] Our job now is to embrace technology **without** yielding our humanity. In this final chapter, let's explore how our enduring human qualities will continue to drive progress and how we can all protect and amplify our 'human advantage' in an AI-powered world.

Leading with Heart: Empathy and Emotional Intelligence

If one theme has echoed throughout this book, it's that empathy is our superpower. Emotional intelligence and empathy are often called 'the glue that holds workplace relationships together.'[4] They build trust, resolve conflicts, and form the bedrock of a positive work culture. Empathy is critical for leaders who listen and genuinely understand their team, fostering loyalty and collaboration.[5] It's vital on the front lines too: from managers supporting an employee through a tough time to customer service reps making a client feel seen and heard. AI cannot replicate this. Yes, algorithms can detect a frown or analyse the sentiment of an email, but they *can't feel*. 'True empathy requires intention and – a distinctly human capacity.'

Importantly, empathy isn't just a 'nice-to-have' soft skill; it drives tangible outcomes. Teams with empathic leadership tend to be more engaged, innovative, and inclusive. Empathy creates psychological safety, allowing people to express ideas and take risks without fear, which fuels creativity. It also underpins well-being, as employees who feel understood and valued report less stress and burnout. When leaders lead with heart, people, and performance thrive. Even as AI assists with data-driven decision-making, leadership in an AI age will hinge on human connection. The most successful leaders will be those who balance technological savvy with compassion, using AI to free up time *for* people, not *from* people.[6] They'll use that time to mentor, to inspire, to build inclusive teams and to check in on colleagues' well-being. In the end, what keeps an organisation resilient and united is the human touch – the leader who remembers birthdays, asks about your sick child or rallies everyone in a crisis. No machine can replicate the morale boost of genuine human care. In the AI era, leading with emotional intelligence will be not only enduring, but game-changing.

Creativity and Innovation: Human Imagination Unleashed

If empathy is the heart, creativity is the spark of human progress. We've learnt that innovation flourishes when we combine human imagination with machine capabilities. AI can be a brilliant tool, analysing data at lightning speed, suggesting patterns, or even drafting rough ideas. In fact, 83 per cent of workers believe AI will enhance human creativity and lead to new forms of value. Instead of fearing AI as a creative rival, we can welcome it as a collaborator that takes over mundane tasks and amplifies our creative potential. By automating the drudgery, AI gives our imaginations room to soar. It might even nudge us with surprising insights, a bit like a brainstorming partner offering wild cards for us to riff on.

The true creative leap still depends on humans. Only people can dream, question assumptions, and dare to try the 'foolish' idea no one's thought of before. As one expert put it, 'AI can generate ideas, but it doesn't have humans' thoughts and dreams.'[7] Our creativity is 'more than recognising patterns or remixing past work' – it's about intuition, emotion and sometimes taking leaps of faith. We have messy, rich inner lives, shaped by personal experiences and cultural context, which spark original ideas that *move* people. AI lacks the spark of a soul. In fact, as AI systems increasingly train on their own outputs (like an echo chamber), truly novel creativity becomes an even more prized human asset. Our quirky, curious, irrational human minds wander off-script – and that's where breakthroughs are born.

We see this in innovative teams: the best ideas often emerge from diverse people bouncing off each other, drawing on empathy (to understand user needs) and imagination (to envision bold solutions). Diversity matters here, as a group of varied humans will out-create a homogenous group *or* a lone algorithm. No wonder research finds that organisations with inclusive cultures are six times more innovative and agile than their less inclusive peers.[8]

In the future, even as AI provides creative inputs, it will be human creativity, guided by our values and insights, that turns those inputs into meaningful innovations.

The enduring power of being human means that *we* remain the ultimate source of art, storytelling, design, and discovery. By embracing AI as a creative catalyst while holding tight to our imagination and judgement, we unlock the best of both worlds – faster breakthroughs powered by technology, grounded in human originality and purpose.

Resilience and Adaptability: Thriving Through Change

Change is already here, and it's constant. Recent shifts, from global pandemics to AI advancements, show how adaptable humans are. Our ability to learn, persevere, and thrive through uncertainty is a key advantage. While machines analyse data, humans use hope, creativity, and grit to navigate challenges and seize opportunities.

Resilience often comes from adversity; each setback strengthens our ability to bounce back. Unlike algorithms, we feel frustration, hope, and the drive to reflect, reinvent and pivot when needed. Resilience is uniquely human, allowing us to turn crises into breakthroughs. We make decisions with incomplete data, empathise with others and stay sane under pressure. AI may follow rules, but we rewrite them when necessary. As one writer noted, AI handles the expected, while we thrive in the unpredictable. Disruption sparks innovation, while human resilience combined with technology achieves remarkable results.

In the workplace, fostering resilience means creating an environment where failure is safe, well-being is supported, and adaptability is encouraged. Organisations that treat employees as partners rather than rigid cogs will thrive. A connected team, where members feel supported, is stronger and more innovative. Collaborative resilience, fuelled by empathy and creativity, will continue to drive progress, no matter how much technology evolves. With adaptability and resilience, we will keep turning challenges into opportunities to grow.

Inclusion and Connection: Powering Culture and Growth

Throughout this book, we emphasised that progress isn't true progress unless it's inclusive. Inclusion, ensuring everyone is valued and heard, is both a moral imperative and a key driver of innovation and growth. As AI takes centre stage, we must not forget the people. This chapter reaffirms that people, in all their diversity, are any organisation's greatest asset. By fostering inclusive leadership and cultures, we unlock the full range of human potential.

Inclusive cultures create a sense of belonging, boosting performance. When people feel safe to be themselves at work, they contribute more effectively and creatively. Research shows that organisations with inclusive cultures are eight times more likely to achieve better outcomes and twice as likely to meet financial targets.[9] Diversity of perspective leads to better problem-solving and new market insights. In the AI era, human diversity is the secret that algorithms can't replicate. While AI provides data, a diverse team brings context and cultural relevance.

Social connection is equally crucial. Humans are wired to connect, and this need doesn't fade in a tech-driven workplace. A survey found that 76 per cent of employees want more human connection as AI grows.[10] People don't want to be treated as replaceable; they want to feel part of a community. Workplaces with strong human connections outperform impersonal, machine-like environments. Strong connections boost collaboration, morale, and mental health, while also protecting against burnout. Inclusion and connection directly impact performance and adaptability.

In the future, inclusive growth will be key to success. Will AI benefit everyone or just a few? That depends on the choices we make. Inclusive leaders will use AI to enhance their teams, close skill gaps, and offer opportunities, not eliminate jobs. They will also guard against AI biases, as algorithms can perpetuate inequality. Human judgement is needed to ensure fairness, with diverse teams auditing AI for inclusivity. By doing this, we can create a future where AI-driven growth benefits all.

The human advantage in inclusion lies in our commitment to justice and equity to ensure no one is left behind. By nurturing this impulse, we can use AI to broaden economic participation and empower communities worldwide. In an automated age, focusing on inclusion is how we build organisations that are not only successful but worthy of success.

A Human-Centred Future: Our Advantage in an AI World

What does all this mean for the future? It means that as we embrace advanced AI, we must keep humanity at the centre. The future will belong to those who combine technology with empathy, data with creativity, and efficiency with ethics. Companies investing in human skills like empathy, creativity, and adaptability are the ones that thrive; they 'future-proof' their workforce and create vibrant, human-centric workplaces. Those that prioritise automation over people risk hollow organisations where employees feel like machines, and these rarely succeed long term. Our competitive advantage is not out-computing computers, but excelling at what they cannot do.

The most successful enterprises of tomorrow will integrate AI across departments, but still feature passionate brainstorming, empathetic leadership, cross-cultural dialogue, and purposeful decision-making.

AI doesn't replace jobs; it enhances them when paired with the right skills. For example, in the insurance industry, AI providing data insights combined with human empathy led to increased customer satisfaction and retention. This winning formula of automation plus human value leads to better outcomes. In healthcare, AI can detect a tumour, but it's a doctor who delivers the news with compassion. AI personalises lesson plans in education, while teachers provide motivation and mentorship. In creative fields, AI might generate drafts, but a human artist adds voice and vision. The key takeaway is that human qualities enhance AI's impact. As a WEF report stated, focusing solely on AI while neglecting humans risks devaluing human capital, while nurturing both ensures we remain in control of progress.[11]

Cultivating Your Human Advantage

Ultimately, the enduring power of being human is a gift and a responsibility. It's something we all must actively cultivate and protect. As individuals, we can commit to growing these critical human skills, and as leaders or organisations, we can create environments that elevate (rather than suppress) our humanity. Here are a few practical ways forward to **cultivating your human advantage** in an AI world:

Practise Empathy Daily

Make a habit of truly listening and understanding others' perspectives. Whether it's a colleague, customer, or friend, give them your full attention. This strengthens your emotional intelligence 'muscle' and builds trust in your relationships. Empathy is contagious. Your example will encourage others to show they care as well.

Embrace Lifelong Learning and Adaptability

Treat new technologies and changes not as threats, but as opportunities to learn. Stay curious. Take that course on AI, try out the new tool, and experiment with different roles. By continually updating your skills and being open to change, you become more resilient and invaluable. Cultivate a mindset that sees change as the norm and adapts proactively.

Unleash Your Creativity

Carve out time for creative thinking and invite diverse ideas. Don't be afraid to brainstorm wildly or pursue a passion project. If you're a leader, set up 'innovation labs' or hackathons for your team and reward original thinking. Remember that creativity isn't just for artists; it can be as simple as finding a new way to streamline a process or solve a customer's problem. Give yourself and others permission to imagine and play.

Lead (and Live) with Values

In your decisions, put people before process and principles before profit. For leaders, this means establishing clear ethical guidelines for how you use AI and data and empowering employees to speak up if something doesn't align with their values. For everyone, it means acting with integrity even when it's hard. Let your moral compass guide your work. This builds a culture of trust and inclusion that no competitor can easily copy.

Foster Inclusion and Connection

Go out of your way to include diverse voices in discussions and decision-making. Seek someone else's viewpoint. Mentor someone from a different background, invest time in building genuine connections, celebrate team wins, have informal chats, and show appreciation. An inclusive, connected culture not only makes work more enjoyable but also unlocks the full potential of your team's talents and perspectives.

Take Care of Well-Being

Finally, remember that humans are not machines, and that's strength. Encourage a healthy work-life balance for yourself and others. Resilience is bolstered when people have the chance to rest, reflect and recharge. Promote wellness initiatives, normalise taking breaks and holidays, and show compassion for mental health. A workforce that feels cared for will bring far more energy, loyalty, and creativity to the table. Protecting our human advantage means protecting the humans themselves.

Each of these actions helps ensure that in the race towards high-tech advancement, we never lose sight of the *human* at the centre. By honing empathy, creativity, critical thinking, and inclusion, we 'future-proof', not just our careers but our sense of purpose. We also make our organisations more agile, innovative and ready to harness AI in the right ways.

A Hopeful, Human-Centred Vision Emerges

Imagine workplaces where AI does the heavy lifting, while humans do the heart work and brain work that we are hardwired for. Imagine workplaces where mundane reports are handled by an AI assistant, freeing employees to brainstorm the next big strategy or to spend an extra hour talking with a client to really understand their needs. Imagine public services where AI quickly analyses data to flag issues, while human experts collaborate on compassionate solutions tailored to communities. Imagine global efforts where AI models climate scenarios, while diverse teams of humans negotiate and implement responses that account for social realities and ethics. In all these scenarios, it's the partnership of technology's power with humanity's guidance that creates progress.

As we conclude *The Human Advantage*, take pride in the qualities you possess; qualities that no algorithm can replicate. Our empathy, creativity, resilience and integrity have carried us through millennia of challenges and will carry us forward into the future. The coming years will undoubtedly surprise us with new innovations, but they will also undoubtedly continue to prove the value of being human. The human spirit – curious, caring, and courageous – is the ultimate renewable resource driving our world.

So, as you finish this book and step into tomorrow, remember that you have something special inside you that every robot would envy (if it could). You have a beating heart, a questioning mind, and an indomitable spirit. Nurture those gifts. In the grand tapestry of progress, your humanity is your edge. It's what will help you lead boldly, connect deeply with others, adapt swiftly to change, and imagine a better future into existence. This is the enduring power of being human that will always, always matter.

'In the end, it is our irreplaceable humanity – our empathy, creativity, and courage – that will light the way forward.'
—Rabi Atiti.

Your humanness is not a flaw to overcome. It is a strength the world needs more than ever.

Acknowledgements

This book could not exist without the unwavering support of my inner circle, my circle of influence, family, friends, mentors, and advisers, whose generosity of time, wisdom, prayers, and encouragement sustained me every step of the way.

I am endlessly grateful for my children, whose patience, curiosity, and sense of wonder inspire me more than they'll ever know. Their voices, laughter, and questions shaped some of these pages in ways that acknowledgements alone cannot contain.

My gratitude will be incomplete without my friends, who believed in this vision before it was fully formed. Thank you for challenging my ideas with candour and compassion. Your faith in me and prayers propelled me forward. I don't take it for granted.

Neil and Hazel Pattison, your leadership has been a guiding light. In your service to humanity, you demonstrate daily what it means to lead God's people with both strength and grace. My family and I are deeply grateful for the gift of your mentorship and the love you share so freely.

Sally Ashford, it was at that dinner in Dubai in October 2023 when you casually asked, 'Have you started writing your book? I think you should.' Your question landed with unexpected clarity and set this journey in motion. This book exists in part because you saw its potential before I did. I am grateful. Thank you!

Lord Stephen A. Carter, your leadership, and unwavering generosity of time have been nothing short of transformative. The wisdom you share, whether in moments of quiet counsel or in stirring calls to action, continues to illuminate our path. You not only teach us what it means to lead with intention and integrity, but also demonstrate how empathy and vision can reshape entire organisations and communities. Thank you for investing your insight into this work. Your influence inspires us to reach higher and reminds us that true leadership transcends titles and transcends boundaries.

A heartfelt thank you to my advance copy readers. Thank you for taking the time to share your generous and thoughtful endorsements of *The Human Advantage*. Your words have added immense value and depth to this book, and I am honoured to feature your voices.

Special appreciation goes to my editor and publisher for her meticulous attention, guidance, and dedication to bringing this vision to life.

I'm incredibly grateful to have shared this journey with you all.

Appendix

The Global Landscape of AI Acts and Regulatory Frameworks – (Source: ChatGPT)

This appendix provides a snapshot of key AI-related laws, guidelines, and regulatory approaches across major global regions. As governments and international organisations respond to the rapid development of artificial intelligence, a range of frameworks have emerged – ranging from binding legislation to voluntary principles. The summaries below highlight notable efforts to address the ethical, legal, and societal implications of AI, with a focus on transparency, accountability, fairness, and human rights.

Europe

- **EU AI Act (European Union)**

    ○ Comprehensive, risk-based framework categorising AI into prohibited, high-risk, limited-risk, and minimal-risk uses. High-risk AI includes applications like hiring, law enforcement, facial recognition, healthcare, and credit scoring. Compliance and transparency are key principles.

- **UK AI Regulation (United Kingdom)**

    ○ Pro-innovation, principles-based approach. Rather than specific legislation, the UK has proposed context-specific guidelines emphasising transparency, fairness, accountability, and robustness in AI systems.

North America
- **U.S. Blueprint for an AI Bill of Rights (United States)**

    ○ Framework emphasising transparency, fairness, privacy protections, and the right to opt out from AI-driven decisions, especially affecting safety-critical sectors like healthcare, hiring, finance, and criminal justice.

- **Algorithmic Accountability Act (United States)**

    ○ Proposed legislation aimed at increasing transparency and accountability of automated decision-making systems used by large companies.

- **Canadian Directive on Automated Decision-Making (Canada)**

    ○ Requires transparency, accountability, and fairness in AI tools used by federal government institutions. Explicitly addresses the potential biases and discriminatory outcomes of automated decisions.

Asia-Pacific

- **China AI Regulation (China)**

  ○ Comprehensive regulatory guidelines and draft laws covering algorithm transparency, ethics, user rights, data protection, and oversight of facial recognition technologies. The rules focus heavily on AI content recommendation algorithms.

- **Singapore Model AI Governance Framework (Singapore)**

  ○ A voluntary, principles-based governance model emphasising transparency, accountability, fairness, human-centricity, and explainability.

- **Australia's AI Ethics Principles (Australia)**

  ○ Principles-based guidelines focused on human rights, fairness, transparency, accountability, and privacy, mainly to guide government and corporate AI implementation.

Middle East and Africa

- **UAE AI Strategy 2031 (United Arab Emirates)**

  ○ A national strategic framework emphasising responsible AI deployment, transparency, and AI-driven public service improvement.

- **South Africa AI Policy (South Africa)**
  - Early-stage development; focus includes ethical deployment, transparency, fairness, and avoiding bias in automated decision-making.

Global and Multilateral Initiatives
- **OECD Principles on AI**
  - A multilateral ethical framework endorsed by 42 countries, promoting responsible stewardship, transparency, fairness, accountability, human rights, and democratic values.

- **UNESCO Recommendation on the Ethics of AI**
  - A global standard promoting human-centred AI that respects human rights, ethical standards, diversity, privacy, and inclusiveness.

ENDNOTES

The Myth of Inevitable Obsolescence

1. The National Archives, *Why Did the Luddites Protest?*, Education – Classroom Resources, https://www.nationalarchives.gov.uk/education/resources/why-did-the-luddites-protest/ (accessed 3 March 2024).

2. American Enterprise Institute, *What ATMs, Bank Tellers & the Rise of Robots Mean for Jobs*, AEI Economics (blog), https://www.aei.org/economics/what-atms-bank-tellers-the-rise-of-robots-mean-for-jobs/ (accessed 7 May 2023).

3. Dennis Holeman, 'The Boeing 737 MAX: A Case Study of Systems Decisions and Their Consequences', *The Systems Perspective* (blog), https://dennisholeman.com/the-boeing-737-max-a-case-study-of-systems-decisions-and-their-consequences/ (accessed 7 May 2023).

4. 'Satya Nadella's Transformation of Microsoft', *Humans of Globe*, https://humansofglobe.com/satya-nadellas-transformation-of-microsoft/ (accessed 4 May 2023).

5. MIT Sloan School of Management, 'When Humans and AI Work Best Together — and When Each Is Better Alone', Ideas Made to Matter, https://mitsloan.mit.edu/ideas-made-to-matter/when-humans-and-ai-work-best-together-and-when-each-better-alone (accessed 7 May 2023).

6. Shabana Azami, 'Fostering Employee Engagement and Retention through Ohana Culture: A Case Study of Salesforce', Kronika Journal 24, no. 7 (2024): 58–65, PDF, https://kronika.ac/wp-content/uploads/6_KKJ2077.pdf (accessed 3 May 2023).

The Business Case for Humanity

1. Gallup, 'The Powerful Relationship Between Employee Engagement and Team Performance', Q^{12} Meta Analysis Executive Brief (2020), https://www.gallup.com/workplace/321032/q12-meta-analysis-executive-brief-2020.aspx (accessed 2 May 2023).

2. Dame Vivian Hunt et al., *Diversity Matters Even More: The Case for Holistic Impact*, McKinsey & Company, 7 January 2024, https://www.mckinsey.com/featured-insights/diversity-and-inclusion/diversity-matters-even-more-the-case-for-holistic-impact (accessed 5 May 2024).

3. Roger Dooley, "The Secret Sauce That Drives Costco's Customer Loyalty" Forbes, 26 June 2024 https://www.forbes.com/sites/rogerdooley/2024/06/26/the-secret-sauce-that-drives-costcos-customer-loyalty/ (accessed 5 May 2023).

4. Gallup, *'Leadership With LUV: Lessons From Southwest Airlines' CEO'*, *Gallup Workplace*, n.d., https://www.gallup.com/workplace/352802/leadership-luv-lessons-southwest-airlines-ceo.aspx (accessed 23 June 2025).

5. Vineet Nayar, *Employees First, Customers Second* (Harvard Business Review Press, 8 June 2010).

6. Deloitte Insights, '2024 Global Human Capital Trends: Thriving beyond boundaries – Human performance in a boundaryless world' (Deloitte, published March 2024) https://www2.deloitte.com/content/dam/insights/articles/glob176836_global-human-capital-trends-2024/DI_Global-Human-Capital-Trends-2024.pdf.

7. World Health Organization, *'Mental Health at Work'*, fact sheet, updated March 2024, https://www.who.int/news-room/fact-sheets/detail/mental-health-at-work (accessed 20 June 2025).

8. Deloitte, Human Sustainability Analytics, 7 November 2023, https://www.deloitte.com/uk/en/services/consulting-risk/perspectives/human-sustainability-analytics.html.

9. *Fortune*, *'Why Jack Welch is Winning'*, 25 January 1993.

The Real Competitive Edge

1. Steven Bartlett, 'AI Agents Emergency Debate: These Jobs Won't Exist', Apple Podcasts, 12 May 2025, https://podcasts.apple.com/az/podcast/ai-agents-emergency-debate-these-jobs-wont-exist (accessed 6 May 2023).

2. 'Lessons From Google's 20 per cent Policy', *Conversational Leadership*, 18 December 2024, https://conversational-leadership.net/google-free-time-policy/ (accessed 4 July 2025).

3. The World Economic Forum, 'The Business Case for Diversity in the Workplace is Now Overwhelming', World Economic Forum, 3 April 2019, https://www.weforum.org/stories/2019/04/business-case-for-diversity-in-the-workplace/.

4. Max SlaterRobins, '15 Inspirational Quotes from Steve Jobs on Life and Work', *Business Insider*, 29 September 2015 https://www.businessinsider.com/steve-jobs-quotes-life-advice-2015-9 (accessed 17 March 2023).

Leading with Humanity in the Digital Age

1. 'McDonald's All Day Breakfast Is Succeeding', *Fortune*, 9 December 2015, https://fortune.com/2015/12/09/mcdonalds-all-day-breakfa st-sales/ (accessed 3 March 2023).

2. IBM, 'How Watson for Oncology Is Advancing Cancer Care', *IBM Newsroom*, 5 October 2017.

3. Autodesk, 'Airbus Uses Generative Design for Lighter, Stronger Aircraft Components', *Autodesk News*, 1 August 2018, https://adsknews.autodesk.com/news/airbus-generative-design (accessed 17 April 2024).

The Future of Leadership

1. Juliet Bourke and Bernadette Dillon, 'The Diversity and Inclusion Revolution: Eight Powerful Truths' Deloitte Review No 22 (22 January 2018 https://www2.deloitte.com/content/dam/insights/us/articles/4209 _Diversity-and-inclusion-revolution/DI_Diversity-and-inclusion-re volution.pdf.

2. Harvard T.H.Chan School of Public Health, How Jacinda Ardern Tackled Public Health Crises in New Zealand https://hsph.harvard.edu/news/how-jacinda-ardern-tackl ed-public-health-crises-in-new-zealand/ (accessed 11 June 2025).

3. Matthew Boyle, *'How Indra Nooyi Built Pepsi for the Future'*, *CNN Money*, 7 August 2018, https://money.cnn.com/2018/08/06/news /companies/indra-nooyi-pepsi/index.html (accessed 2 June 2025).

4. Patagonia, *'1% for the Planet'*, https://www.patagonia.com/one-pe rcent-for-the-planet/ (accessed 11 June 2025).

5. *'A Year After Christchurch, Jacinda Ardern Has the World's Attention'*, *Time*, 20 February 2020, https://time.com/5780834/jacinda-ardern-christchurch-anniversary/ (accessed 7 June 2025).

6. Premium Times Nigeria, *'Beneficiaries Receive $5,000 Each as Tony Elumelu Foundation Announces 2024 Cohort'*, 24 March 2024, https://www.premiumtimesng.com/news/more-news/680282-benef iciaries-receive-5000-each-as-tony-elumelu-foundation-announces-2024-cohort.html (accessed 2 May 2024).

7. Mfonobong Nsehe, 'Meet Tony Elumelu, Africa's Frontline Business Leader', Forbes, 9 January 2012, https://www.forbes.com/sites/mfonobongnsehe/2012/01/0 9/meet-tony-elumelu-africas-frontline-business-leader/ (accessed 24 May 2024).

8. Tony Elumelu Foundation, 'About Us', https://www.tonyelumeluf oundation.org/about-us (accessed 11 June 2025).

9. Sophie Wingate, "The Nation Is Using Collective Intelligence to Address Social Needs, Audrey Tang Tells Summit," Global Solutions Initiative, May 28, 2021.

10. Megan Molteni, *"Taiwan's Digital Minister Knows How to Crush Covid19: Trust"*, WIRED, 23 July 2020, https://www.wired.com/story/wired25-day3-audrey-tang-taiwan/ (accessed 24 July 2025).

11. Ricardo Semler, Maverick! The Success Story Behind the World's Most Unusual Workplace (New York: Warner Books, 1993).

12. Erin McCormick, *"Patagonia's Billionaire Owner Gives Away Company to Fight Climate Crisis"*, The Guardian, 14 September 2022, https://www.theguardian.com/us-news/2022/sep/14/patagonias-bi llionaire-owner-gives-away-company-to-fight-climate-crisis-yvon-chouinard (accessed 24 March 2025).

Emotional Intelligence

1. Daniel Goleman, *Emotional Intelligence: Why It Can Matter More Than IQ* (New York: Bantam Books, 1995).

2. "It's Cool to Be Kind: The Value of Empathy at Work", McKinsey Talks Talent, 28 February 2024, https://www.mckinsey.com/capabilities/people-and-organisational-performance/our-insights/its-cool-to-be-kind-the-value-of-empathy-at-work (accessed 11 March 2024).

3. Côté and Miners, "Emotional Intelligence, Cognitive Intelligence, and Job Performance"; Gallup, State of the Global Workplace, 2022.

4. Hamdi Ulukaya, 'Chobani Founder Hamdi Ulukaya on the Journey from Abandoned Factory to Yogurt Powerhouse', Harvard Business Review, 25 April 2022 https://hbr.org/2022/04/chobani-founder-hamdi-ulukaya-on-the-journey-from-abandoned-factory-to-yogurt-powerhouse (accessed 4 July 2025).

5. Jena McGregor, 'Chobani's CEO Is Giving up to 10 Percent of His Company to Employees', *The Washington Post*, 27 April 2016 (accessed 3 July 2025).

6. Kakenya Ntaiya, 'I Survived Female Genital Mutilation — Now, I Fight to Ensure No Other Girl Has to Suffer', *Global Citizen* (accessed 5 July 2025).

7. The School of We, "Search Inside Yourself Program," The School of We (accessed 13 June 2025).

8. "The Role of Emotional Intelligence Assessments on Executive Performance Measurement," Smart 360 Feedback, (accessed June 2025).

9. Amy Gallo, "What Is Psychological Safety?", Harvard Business Review, 15 February 2023, Harvard Business Review (hbr.org), (accessed 7 March 2024).

10. Nick Hobson, "Airbnb CEO Brian Chesky Tells Adam Grant the Right Way to Do Mass Layoffs: 'Cut Deep,'" Inc.com, May 25, 2024.

The Global Power of Inclusion

1. Safaricom Recognized as the Most Inclusive Listed Company in Kenya, press release, 9 March 2023;Realising that traditional corporate structures excluded women, people with disabilities and rural communities, Safaricom redesigned its internal systems.

2. P. Christopher Earley and Soon Ang, Cultural Intelligence: Individual Interactions across Cultures (Stanford: Stanford University Press, 2003).

3. Tsedal Neeley, "How to Successfully Work Across Countries, Languages, and Cultures," Harvard Business Review, August 29, 2017.

4. CEO, Natura. Daniela Ferreira, *'Natura Shares Its Vision of Sustainability', Happi*, 16 October 2023, (accessed 24 July 2025).

5. Emirates Group, *'Working with Us', The Emirates Group Careers*. (accessed 7 May 2025).

6. Deloitte, 'New Deloitte Research Identifies Keys to Creating Fair and Inclusive Organisations', *PR Newswire*, 19 March 2020 https://www.prnewswire.com/news-releases/new-deloitte-research-identifies-keys-to-creating-fair-and-inclusive-organisations-301025351.html (accessed 24 July 2025).

Agility Versus Burnout

1. Mercer, Global Talent Trends 2024–2025, Global Talent Trends report (New York: Mercer, 2024).

2. Samuel Hussey, "From One Disaster to the Next': Inside the Great Australian Burnout," Forbes Australia, n.d., (accessed 11 June 2025).

3. Deloitte, "Poor Mental Health Costs UK Employers £51 Billion a Year," press release (London: Deloitte UK, 2023).

4. McKinsey & Company, "DBS Bank: Transforming Digital Banking in Singapore," Rewired in Action (blog). https://www.mckinsey.com/capabilities/mckinsey-digital/how-we-help-clients/rewired-in-action/dbs-transforming-a-banking-leader-into-a-technology-leader.

5. Aon and TELUS Health, Asia Mental Health Index Report 2023, September 14, 2023, https://www.telus.com/en/health/resource-centre/content/asia-mental-health-index-report-2023.

6. Aon plc, 'The Next Evolution of Wellbeing Is About Performance', Aon Insights, 3 March 2023, Aon plc, (accessed 3 June 2025).

7. Paulina Modlitba, *"Fika Time: The Swedish Coffee Break That Might Save Your Company,"* Mint, 11 May 2024 (accessed 14 March 2025).

8. Aon plc, "Aon's Survey Finds Employee Wellbeing Has Risen in Importance and Investment; Mental Health Is Top Wellbeing Issue in Asia Pacific," Malay Mail (Media Outreach), May 3, 2023.

9. '4-day Workweek Pilot in South Africa – The Results Are In' Labour Guide South Africa, March 2023. (Accessed 11 June 2025).

10. 'Sharjah's New Four-Day Work Week Improved Government Performance, Reduced Accidents by 40 per cent, Study Finds', *Gulf News*, 9 August 2022 (accessed 12 July 2024).

11. 'Dominican Republic to Launch Pilot Program Offering a 4-Day Workweek to Public and Private Workers', *AP News*, 16 January 2024 (accessed 24 July 2025).

12. 'Chile Considers Reducing Standard Workweek to Combat Burnout', *Reuters*, 15 March 2024 (accessed 24 July 2025).

13. Jessica Murray, 'UK Four-Day Week Pilot Sees 92 per cent of Firms Continue Reduced Hours', *The Guardian*, 7 December 2023 (accessed 24 July 2025).

14. 'Tackling Work-Life Balance: Microsoft Japan's Four-Day Workweek Boosted Productivity by 40 per cent', *BBC News*, 15 August 2019 (accessed 24 July 2025).

15. Eidos-Montréal, 'Eidos-Montréal and Eidos-Sherbrooke Shifting to the 4-Day Work Week' (accessed 20 March 2025) .

16. Rebecca M. Knight, 'Can AI Help Companies Boost Employee Well-Being?', *Business Insider*, 10 September 2024 (accessed 17 March 2025).

17. New AI-Powered Qualtrics Solutions Empower Leaders to Boost Employee Engagement With Strategic, Informed Action', *Qualtrics*, 30 October 2024 (accessed 24 February 2024).

18. 'AI Provider Matching', *Lyra Health Blog*, 15 March 2021 (accessed 2 July 2025).

19. Benjamin Laker, Vijay Pereira, Pawan Budhwar and Ashish Malik, 'The Surprising Impact of Meeting Free Days', *MIT Sloan Management Review*, 18 January 2022 (accessed 2 July 2025).

20. Olivier Picquerey and Claire Toumieux, 'The New "Right to Disconnect" in France', *A&O Shearman via JD Supra*, 23 February 2017 https://www.jdsupra.com/legalnews/the-new-right-to-disconnect-in-france-58056/ (accessed 24 July 2025).

21. Emily Rodgers, '5 Powerful HR KPIs for Measuring Organisational Success', *Wellics* (blog), originally published 19 October 2022, updated 3 September 2024 https://www.wellics.com/blog/hr-kpis (accessed 12 May 2025).

22. Psico Smart Editorial Team, 'What Innovative KPIs Can Organisations Implement to Measure Employee Engagement and Productivity in 2023?', Psico Smart Blog, 2 March 2025 https://psicosmart.pro/en/blogs/blog-what-innovative-kpis-can-organisations-implement-to-measure-employee-e-20070 (accessed 10 May 2025).

23. World Health Organisation and International Labour Organisation, Long Working Hours Increasing Deaths from Heart Disease and Stroke: WHO, ILO, press release, 17 May 2021 https://www.who.int/news/item/17-05-2021-long-working-hours-increasing-deaths-from-heart-disease-and-stroke-who-ilo (accessed 24 July 2025).

24. American Psychological Association, 2023 Work in America Survey: Workplace Health and Well-being, 2023, https://www.apa.org/pubs/reports/work-in-america/2023-workplace-health-well-being.

25. Staff Reporter, 'CIMB Bank Singapore Emphasises Employee Engagement', Singapore Business Review, published May 2023 (approximate) https://sbr.com.sg/co-written-partner/event-news/cimb-bank-singapore-emphasises-employee-engagement.

Resilience and Reinvention

1. Elle Wong, 'Learning Agility: The Cornerstone of Modern Recruitment and HR', *Adaface Blog* https://www.adaface.com/blog/learni ng-agility/ (accessed 24 July 2025).

2. Nassim Nicholas Taleb, Antifragile: Things That Gain from Disorder (New York: Random House, 2012).

3. 'Bhavini Mehta Success Story', *eShe* (blog), 21 October 2017 https:/ /eshe.in/2017/10/21/bhavini-mehta-success-story/ (accessed 24 July 2025).

4. Carol S. Dweck, Mindset: The New Psychology of Success (New York: Random House, 2006).

5. Netflix: "How a DVD Rental Company Changed the Way We Spend Our Free Time," *Business Models Inc.* (blog) https://www.businessmodelsinc.com/en/inspiration/blogs/netflix-how-a-dvd-rental-company-changed-the-way-we-spend-our-free-time.

6. Elle Wong, "Learning Agility: The Cornerstone of Modern Recruitment and HR," *Adaface Blog* (published date not listed), https://www.adaface.com/blog/learning-agility/#:~:text=Learning%20agility%20is%20a%20predictor%E2%80%A6.

7. Alec Ross, The Raging 2020s: Companies, Countries, People – and the Fight for Our Future (London: John Murray, 2021).

8. Nancy Koehn, Forged in Crisis: The Power of Courageous Leadership in Turbulent Times (New York: Scribner, 2017).

Designing the Future of Work Around Humans

1. McKinsey & Company, "Shattering the Status Quo: A Conversation on Organisational Transformation", *McKinsey & Compa-ny*, https://www.mckinsey.com/capabilities/people-and-organisational-performance/our-insights/shattering-the-status-quo-a-conve.

2. Art Kleiner and Vikas Sehgal, "The Thought Leader Interview: Vineet Nayar," *strategy+business*, October 18, 2010, originally published by Booz & Company, (accessed June 12, 2025), https://www.strategy-business.com/article/10410 .

3. "How Haier Is Shattering the Status Quo: A Conversation with Haier's Zhang Ruimin," *McKinsey & Company*, https://www.mckinsey.com/capabilities/people-and-organisational-performance/our-insights/shattering-the-status-quo-a-conversation-with-haiers-zhang-ruimin .

4. Timothy R. Clark (CEO, LeaderFactor), "Google's Project Aristotle Was the Most Important Study on Team Effectiveness in a Generation," *LinkedIn*, posted September 2024 (accessed 12 June 2025). https://www.linkedin.com/posts/timothyrclark_googles-project-aristotle-was-the-most-important-activity-72393028053357 .

5. Holger Reisinger and Dane Fetterer, "Forget Flexibility. Your Employees Want Autonomy," *Harvard Business Review*, October 29, 2021, https://hbr.org/2021/10/forget-flexibility-your-employees-want-autonomy.

6. Deloitte, *Global Human Capital Trends 2014: Engaging the 21st Century Workforce*, Deloitte In-sights, https://www2.deloitte.com/us/en/insights/focus/human-capital-trends/2014/hc-trends-2014-performance-manage.

7. Gallup and Workhuman, "The Human Centred Workplace: Building Organisational Cultures That Thrive."

8. *Deloitte Insights*, February 28, 2015, https://www2.deloitte.com/us/en/insights/focus/human-capital-trends/2015/performance-management-redesign-human-capital-trends-2015.html.

9. Stuart Tucker, "Employee Experience | How John Lewis & Partners Improved Staff Satisfaction and Earned £1.5 Million," *Princess Royal Training Awards* (blog), January 22, 2019, https://princessroyaltrainingawards.com/2019/01/employee-experie nce-how-john-lewis-partners-improved-staff-satisfaction-and-earned-1-5million/.

10. American Psychological Association, "2023 Work in America Survey: Workplace Health & Well Being," *Work in America Survey Reports*, https://www.apa.org/pubs/reports/work-in-america/2023-w orkplace-health-well-being.

11. **Spill**, "Mental Health Statistics – Workplace Mental Health Statistics," *Spill.chat*, https://www.spill.chat/mental-health-statistics/wo rkplace-mental-health-statistics .

12. Lyra Health, "Choosing a Mental Health Benefit: What to Look For," *Lyra Health* (blog), https://www.lyrahealth.com/blo g/choosing-a-mental-health-benefit/.

13. Volkswagen, "Volkswagen Turns Off BlackBerry Email After Work Hours," *BBC News*, March 15, 2012 (UK) https://www.bbc.com/n ews/technology-16314901.

14. Ellen Ernst Kossek, Patricia Gettings, and Kaumudi Misra, "The Future of Flexibility at Work," *Harvard Business Review*, September 28, 2021, https://hbr.org/2021/09/the-future-of-flexibility-at-work .

15. Atlassian. "Distributed Work." *Atlassian*, (accessed 12 June 2025) https://www.atlassian.com/solutions/distributed.

16. Zoom (in partnership with Reworked INSIGHTS), "Zoom Survey Reveals Hybrid Work Reigns Supreme and Delivers Unexpected Value to Global Organisations," *Zoom News*, August 26, 2024, https://news.zoom.com/zoom-survey-reveals-hybrid-work-reigns-supreme-and-delivers-unexpected-value-to-global-organisations/.

17. The Five Echelon Group, "What Are Results Only Work Environments (ROWE)?" *The Five Echelon Group* (blog), March 2, 2023, https://fiveechelon.com/results-only-work-environment/.

18. BBC, "Four day Week 'an Overwhelming Success' in Iceland," *BBC News*, July 6, 2021, https://www.bbc.com/news/business-57724779.

19. *The Guardian*, November 4, 2019, https://www.theguardian.com/technology/2019/nov/04/microsoft-japan-four-day-work-week-productivity.

20. BBC, "Thousands of UK Workers Begin World's Biggest Trial of Four Day Week," *The Guardian*, June 6, 2022, https://www.theguardian.com/business/2022/jun/06/thousands-workers-worlds-biggest-trial-four-day-week.

21. Patty McCord, "How Netflix Reinvented HR," *Harvard Business Review*, January–February 2014, (accessed 12 June 2025) https://hbr.org/2014/01/how-netflix-reinvented-hr.

22. Advisory.com, "What Your Hybrid Employees Actually Need (Hint: It Isn't 'Flexibility.')," *Advisory*, November 1, 2021, (accessed June 12, 2025) https://www.advisory.com/daily-briefing/2021/11/01/employee-autonomy.

23. BBC, "Four Day Week 'an Overwhelming Success' in Iceland," *BBC News*, July 6, 2021, https://www.bbc.com/news/business-57724779.

Time Together: An Informa Case Study

1. Barbara Jeffery, Brooke Weddle, Jacqueline Brassey, and Shail Thaker, *"Thriving Workplaces: How Employers Can Improve Productivity and Change Lives*, McKinsey Health Institute in collaboration with the World Economic Forum, January 16, 2025, https://www.mckinsey.com/mhi/our-insights/thriving-workplaces-how-employers-can-improve-productivity-and-change-lives.

2. Lauren Doherty, "Leading in a Hybrid World," *Harvard Business Publishing* (blog), January 20, 2023, https://www.harvardbusiness.org/insight/leading-in-a-hybrid-world/.

Building Psychological Resilience

1. American Psychological Association, Building Your Resilience (APA, 2024) https://www.apa.org/topics/resilience/building-your-resilience (accessed 4 May 2025).

2. Bill Burnett and Dave Evans, Designing Your Life: How to Build a Well Lived, Joyful Life (New York: Knopf, 2016).

3. Sean Carney, PA, MBA, PCC, LinkedIn post, *"The Reinvention Sprint™: 4 Week Hybrid Caching Program"*, https://www.linkedin.com/posts/carneysean_the-reinvention-sprint-4-week-hybrid-coaching-activity-7272620251832360960%E2%80%91NU_Q.

4. Our Heritage," *Fiskars*, https://www.fiskars.com/en/about-us/our-heritage.

5. David C Robertson with Bill Breen, Brick by Brick: How LEGO Rewrote the Rules of Innovation and Conquered the Toy Industry (Crown Business 2013).

6. Duhigg, Charles. "What Google Learned from Its Quest to build the Perfect Team." *New York Times Magazine*, February 28, 2016. https://www.nytimes.com/2016/02/28/magazine/what-google-learned-from-its-quest-to-build-the-perfect-team.html.

7. John Donovan and Cathy Benko, "AT&T's Talent Overhaul," *Harvard Business Review*, October 2016, https://hbr.org/2016/10/atts-talent-overhaul.

8. Mike Bechtel and Nishita Henry, *Innovation Study 2021: Beyond the Buzzword* (Deloitte Insights, September 30, 2021), https://www2.deloitte.com/content/dam/insights/articles/US164607_CIO-Innovation-and-ecosystem-study/DI_CIO-Innovation-and-ecosystem-study.pdf.

9. McKinsey & Company, "Shattering the Status Quo: A Conversation on Organisational Transformation," *McKinsey & Company*, (accessed 12 June 2025) https://www.mckinsey.com/capabilities/people-and-organisational-performance/our-insights/shattering-the-status-quo-a-conver .

10. One Sasol SHE Excellence Approach (Sasol, 2023) https://www.sasol.com/sites/default/files/2023-08/9.15%20%20One%20Sasol%20SHE%20Excellence%20Approach_0_1.pdf (accessed 4 March 2024).

11. Louis V. Gerstner Jr., "IBM's Transformation in the 1990s: The Rise of EBusiness," *Eustochos*, (accessed 12 June 2025) https://eustochos.com/ibms-transformation-in-the-1990s/.

12. Rita McGrath, "Failure Is a Gold Mine for India's Tata," *Harvard Business Review*, April 11, 2011, https://hbr.org/2011/04/failure-is-a-gold-mine-for-ind.

Leveraging Technology

1. Microsoft, Closed Captions and Transcription | Accessibility | Microsoft Teams (Microsoft, May 2025) https://www.microsoft.com/en%E2%80%91us/microsoft%E2%80%91teams/accessibility%E2%80%91closed%E2%80%91captions%E2%80%91transcriptions (accessed 5 July 2025).

2. Cassie Sanchez, *"Want to hire more women?"*, Textio Blog, published c. January 2024, (accessed 5 July 2025) (https://textio.com/blog/want-to-hire-more-women?utm_source=chatgpt.com.

3. Microsoft Education Team, *"Inclusive design for accessible learning"*, Microsoft Education Blog, 1 December 2022, (accessed 5 July 2025) https://www.microsoft.com/en-us/education/blog/2022/12/inclusive-design-for-accessible-learning/?utm_source=chatgpt.

4. Consultancy.uk, "Accenture Buys 60,000 Oculus Head-sets for VR Training," *Consultancy.uk*, November 5 2021, https://www.consultancy.uk/news/29463/accenture-buys-6 0000-oculus-headsets-for-vr-training.

5. McKinsey & Company, Technology, Media, and Telecom in Europe: The New Growth Engine or Another Decade of Missing Out (Report, 21 May 2025) https://www.mckinsey.com/industries/technology-media-and-telec ommunications/our-insights/technology-media-and-telecom-in-eur ope-the-new-growth-engine-or-another-decade-of-missing-out (accessed 4 July 2025).

6. *The Wellbeing Budget 2019*, The Treasury, New Zealand, May 30, 2019, https://www.treasury.govt.nz/publications/wellbein g-budget/wellbeing-budget%E2%80%912019.

7. Grace Chang, "How Japan Is Healing from It Overwork Crisis through Innovation," *World Economic Forum*, October 18, 2024, https://www.weforum.org/stories/2024/10/japan-ka roshi-overwork-crisis-innovation/.

8. Corporate Rebels, Panelfisa: Innovating Through Decentralized Empowerment (1 July 2024).

9. Eduardo P. Braun, Haier Group: A Case on How Culture Can Fos-ter Product and Management Innovation eduardopbraun.com, (accessed 2 July 2025).

10. Dr Rita Fontinha, Reducing Working Hours in Iceland: Lessons on Workload and Flexibility (Henley Business School, 27 July 2021) https://www.henley.ac.uk/news/2021/reducing-working-hours-in-iceland-lessons-on-workload-and-flexibility (accessed 2 July 2025).

11. Richard Sheridan, "How One CEO Creates Joy at Work," *HBR IdeaCast* (podcast), December 18, 2018, (accessed June 12, 2025), https://hbr.org/podcast/2018/12/how-one-ceo-creates-joy-at-work.

12. *Marks & Spencer Group plc*, "Results Reports, webcasts & Presentations," (accessed June 12, 2025), corporate section, *Marks & Spencer Group plc* investor site, https://corporate.marksandspencer.com/sites/marksandspencer/file s/marks-spencer/results-reports-webcasts-and-presentation/rcf-sustainability-kpi-performance-update-2024 pdf.

Conclusion

1. HTE, "Why Human Skills Are the key to Thriv-ing in an AI Driven Workplace," *HR Tech Edge*, April 3, 2025, https://hrtechedge.com/why-human-skills-are-the-k ey-to-thriving-in-an-ai-driven-workplace.

2. Jim Stratton, "How We Can Elevate Uniquely Human Skills in the Age of AI," *World Economic Forum*, January 2025, https://www.weforum.org/stories/2025/01/elevating-uniquely-human-skills-in-the-age-of-ai.

3. . Piyachart (Arm) Isarabhakdee, "AI Will Drive Growth. But Only Authentic Intelligence Can Empower the World," *World Economic Forum*, March 2025, (accessed 12 June 2025), https://www.weforu m.org/stories/2025/03/ai-authentic-intelligence/.

4. "What AI Can't Take: 5 Traits to Preserve Humanity in the Workplace," *reworked.co*, (accessed 12 June 2025) https://www.reworked.co/employee-experience/what-ai-cant-take-5-traits-to-preserve-humanity-in-the-workplace/.

5. The Five Echelon Group, "What Are Results Only Work Environments (ROWE)?," *The Five Echelon Group* (blog), March 2, 2023, https://fiveechelon.com/results-only-work-environment/.

6. Jim Stratton, "How We Can Elevate Uniquely Human Skills in the Age of AI," *World Economic Forum*, January 2025, https://www.weforum.org/stories/2025/01/elevating-uni quely-human-skills-in-the-age-of-ai/.

7. Our Humanity, Not Technology, Should Lead the Future of Work: What AI Can't Take -5 Traits to Preserve Humanity in the Workplace," *Reworked*, (accessed 3 July 2025) https://www.reworked.co/employee-experience/what-ai-cant-take-5-traits-to-preserve-humanity-in-the-workplace/.

8. Eugene Ivanov, "The Role of Diversity in Innovation," *HeroX*, accessed June 12, 2025, https://www.herox.com/blog/936-the-role-of-diversity-in-innovation.

9. Kim Lessley, 'Fostering an Inclusive Culture Is a Business Imperative, Not a Trend', *Forbes* (15 October 2020) https://www.forbes.com/sites/sap/2020/10/15/fostering-an-inclusive-culture-is-a-business-imperative-not-a-trend/ (accessed 14 May 2023).

10. Gallup, *State of the Global Workplace: 2021 Report* https://www.gallup.com/workplace/349484/state-of-the-global-workplace.aspx (accessed 11 May 2024).

11. Piyachart (Arm) Isarabhakdee, "AI will drive growth. But only Au-thentic Intelligence can empower the world", World Economic Fo-rum, 12 March 2025, World Economic Forum, (accessed 5 July 2025).

Printed in Dunstable, United Kingdom